The Gate to Perfection
The Idea of Peace in Jewish Thought

The Gate to Perfection
The Idea of Peace in Jewish Thought

Walter Homolka
Albert H. Friedlander

With a preface by
Elie Wiesel

Berghahn Books
Providence

Published in 1994 by
Berghahn Books Inc.

British Library Cataloguing in Publication Data
A CIP catalog record for this book is available from
the British Library.

Library of Congress Cataloging-in-Publication Data
Homolka, Walter.
[Von der Sintflut ins Paradies. English]
The gate to perfection : the idea of peace in Jewish thought /
Walter H. Homolka, Albert H. Friedlander : with a
preface by Elie Wiesel.
p.   cm.
Includes bibliographical references.
ISBN 1-57181-018-8 : $29.00
1. Peace—Religious aspects—Judaism.
I. Friedlander, Albert H.   II. Title
BM538.P3H6613   1994   94-22783
296.3'87873—dc20   CIP

Printed in the United States.

In memory of
Steven Schwarzschild
and
Jakob J. Petuchowski
who walked through the
Gate of Peace

"We glorify the source of peace,

for peace is the gate to our perfection,

and in perfection is our rest."

Forms of Prayer for Jewish Worship
London 1977

Contents

Acknowledgments

This book couldn't have been done except for the continuing cooperation of Dr. Jonathan Campbell, lecturer in Jewish Studies at St. David's University College Lampeter, University of Wales (Great Britain).

We are very grateful for the tremendous help of Monika Preuß, Heidelberg, in the editing process of the material presented. Peter Heitmann, the editor of the German original edition at "Wissenschaftliche Buchgesellschaft Darmstadt" (1993) added much clarity when preparing the script for initial publication. So did Robert Riddell who deserves much credit for the process of editing the English version with its revisions and updatings.

Special thanks must also be given to Ms. Alison Brown, Berlin, who translated chapters I to VI. Chapter VII was translated by Dr. William Templer who has also contributed a number of important suggestions which have improved this text.

It may be helpful here to draw the reader's attention to a few points by way of explanation. The Revised Standard Version has been used for English citations from the Bible and Apocrypha, unless otherwise stated. For English citations from the Talmud the Soncino Talmud has been used, unless otherwise stated. I have found it necessary to supply my own translations on occasion.

Homolka, 1994

List of Abbreviations

Deut	Deuteronomy
Deut Rabbah	Deuteronomy Rabbah
Eccles	Ecclesiastes
Ex	Exodus
Ezek	Ezekiel
Gen	Genesis
Gen Rabbah	Genesis Rabbah
Hag	Haggai
Hos	Hosea
Is	Isaiah
Jer	Jeremiah
Josh	Joshua
Judg	Judges
Lev	Leviticus
Lev Rabbah	Leviticus Rabbah
Mic	Micah
Num	Numbers
Num Rabbah	Numbers Rabbah
Prov	Proverbs
Ps	Psalms
Sam	Samuel
trans.	translated

Preface *

Does the history of this bloody century lead from Sarajevo back to Sarajevo? There was a time when we thought that name was an echo from the First World War, and had nothing to do with the present. Perhaps the signs of the times are trying to tell us something: that what passes as civilized life is a constant process of beginning anew. The tragedy currently devastating the former Yugoslavia stands as a warning.

Once again, an ancient scenario is repeated, no matter what the place on the planet: people killing and being killed. On and on. The reasons for such slaughter are always as different as they are insane. And our so-called civilized society permits the carnage to happen, again and again. As in the traumatic aftershock of the Shoah, now again we find ourselves asking whether there are any words adequate to express our horror. And who could we describe it to? Shall the great leaders of the world's nations continue to indulge in the game of playing with grand but hollow phrases, as they did in the time of the Third Reich — instead of acting to prevent the death of ever more innocent victims?

As a Jew and a person who has experienced what it means to be bereft of all help in a time of terrible distress, I believe that we Jews in particular should now raise our voices in indignation, protesting louder than the others. Anyone who does not want to dismiss humanity as but a brief chapter in the history of Central Europe must deal seriously with the longing for peace there. Naturally there is a danger that the old scenarios will be repeated, that ears will remain deaf. We look into the emaciated faces of the prisoners, see streets piled with corpses — the images so profuse that we have become accustomed to them. We are well informed, but not concerned. What we fail to realize is that indifference leads to guilt.

Elie Wiesel

* Authorized by Elie Wiesel from *Die Welt*, 27 October 1992, trans. William Templer.

Introduction

Judaism as a religion characterized by the striving for peace represents the result of a long development which I tried to depict and Albert H. Friedlander uses for his analysis of the Jewish attitude toward and experience with peace in contemporary times.

Our aim was not to give the impression that Jewish history evidences a simple straightforward progression from belief in a primitive war-like god at the beginning (i.e., in early biblical times) to an elevated ideal of a universal peace realm at the end in modern times.

The lethargy in the development of biblical thought before and after the prophets as well as the ironic juxtaposition of Hermann Cohen's concept of universal peace with the beginning of the First World War are two examples that things were, of course, more complicated. There have been obvious regressions, as well as improvement, as time went on.

Nevertheless it was our intention to elaborate some linearity in the development of concepts. Three major shifts were particularly significant in this development:

- The religious nationalism of the Israelites gave way to a religious universalism of Judaism that included all of humanity.

This tendency was even present in Graeco-Roman times. It was suppressed, however, by Jewish-Christian rivalry and the Christian universalism of St. Paul, and could only unfold again after the Enlightenment: on the basis of both Hegelian and Neo-Kantian thought on the one hand and within a pluralistic society on the other.[1]

---

1. See Walter Homolka, "Jewish Religious Identity as a Process of Continuity and Change", in Bruchner, Eckart and Vermeire, Geert (ed.), *Culturen, Religies en Beeld*, Wielsbeke (Belgium), 1993, pp. 20—43.

- The ancient Israelite war-god *"Adonai Zebaoth"* evolved into a god of peace and justice having an influence beyond Judaism and forming the ideas and ideals of a Christian Occident on the basis of its "root Israel."

- Judaism developed the notion of an "enemy with a human face," conceding the so-called "enemy" also to be created in the image of God, thereby rejecting his annihilation, as had previously been sanctioned by the ancient Israelites.

Accordingly, the Jewish concept of peace was never limited to a mere political state of affairs, but rather encompasses:

- Peace in oneself

- Peace with one's neighbors

- Peace in the community,
  and ultimately,

- Peace on earth

World peace especially refers to the ultimate time in which all of this will be achieved, not only among the Jewish people, but among all living things, that is, the whole world. This idea gave rise to all hopes and expectations for a Messianic age and became a concrete ideology for a better society when Jews in Europe obtained the chance of assimilating into the societies of their own nation-states.

Of special importance was the rise of individualism in the Jewish religion, starting with the prophet Jeremia. It became the basis for the whole approach to Torah as presented in the Oral Tradition: focusing on the right conduct of the individual faithful within the community and in the encounter with his creator and sustainer. Now the life and actions of each individual should be directed, according to Jewish thought, toward the realization of this great goal: to hasten the dawning of that which is referred to as the "Messianic Age," which is meant to come in the here-and-now.

> I call heaven and earth to witness against you this day, that I have set before you life and death, blessing and curse; therefore choose life, that you and your descendants may live. (Deut 30.19)

The present volume aims at analyzing the development of the idea of peace in Israel and Judaism from biblical times until the end of the Neo-Kantian influence in modern Jewish thought.

In the first chapter I will elaborate the idea of peace as it is presented in the Hebrew Bible. This part of the study aims at presenting biblical texts as they were traditionally understood by Jewish theology. It does not attempt to classify the selected biblical texts according to the methods of historical criticism. The methods of historical criticism seek to divide the different sources that were intermingled in order to form the national *epos* of a united Israel. The original text is thereby theoretically reconstructed and structured according to distinguishable forms and brought into a historical sequence in order to come to conclusions about the theological developments within the Biblical texts. This approach has never found much reception in Jewish scholarly endeavors to understand Bible and tradition, although the *"Wissenschaft des Judentums"* was aware of the techniques. This may have been partly due to the Christian bias of early historical criticism, which aimed at denigrating the Jewish tradition and the importance of God's Chosen People in contrast to the rise of early Christianity and the evolving rivalry. It was not only Orthodox Jewish scholars who did not take up the ideas of historical criticism, but also less traditionalistic scholars such as Umberto Cassuto.

Jewish biblical exegesis centered much more around the development and growth of explaining the chain of tradition from the canonized set of texts in the Hebrew Bible until modern times (*"Wirkungsgeschichte"*). This study — though not unaware of the achievements of historical criticism — will focus on this Jewish approach.

The second part of the book is dedicated to the *"sefarim chizoniim'"* and the works of Philo and Josephus. In this section the influence on the concept of peace within the Jewish-Hellenistic symbiosis will be worked out. The rise of individualism as a change in Jewish religious thought will be elaborated and its influences, as manifest in the Apocrypha and Pseudepigrapha, will be shown.

In the third section the views on peace in Talmudic Times will be examined. The effects of the destruction of the

Second Temple and the loss of national unity on Jewish religious thought will be studied. The change in the meaning of the term "peace" from "absence of war" to a theological concept has to be shown.

The fourth part deals with medieval Jewish philosophy and its attitude toward peace. The emphasis on the talmudic concept of peace by medieval Jewish scholars will be demonstrated. A short survey on peace in kabbalistic writings is added.

In the fifth section the influences of the Jewish Enlightenment and the Emancipation of the Jews on the concept of peace will be discussed. I will focus on Hasidism and the *"Wissenschaft des Judentums,"* but I found it unnecessary to discuss Neo-orthodoxy, as it did not contribute extraordinary new material to the discussion on peace. The Hasidic movement is rooted in Eastern Europe and with its pure piety and emotional approach to prayer and service became a sort of prototype for eastern Judaism. Moritz Lazarus and his interpretation of the concept of peace is taken as an example of the latter. Thirdly, Hermann Cohen's ethical and moral teachings, as far as they are concerned with "peace," will be discussed. Cohen — the most outstanding representative of the Neo-Kantian Marburg school — had a remarkable influence on modern progressive Jewish theology.

In the part on the Jewish Reformation, Leo Baeck's contribution to the idea of peace in Jewish theology — Baeck being a pupil of Cohen[2] — is chosen as a representative of modern German-Jewish thought.

Finally, Albert H. Friedlander elaborates the Jewish attitude toward peace in the light of the Holocaust and the foundation of the State of Israel.

It is hoped that the book will show the inner development of the concept of peace from the Canon of the Hebrew Bible up to the progressive Judaism of Modern Times: from the idea of peace as "absence of war" to the idea of peace as cosmic harmony.

---

2. See Walter Homolka, *Jüdische Identität in der modernen Welt — Leo Baeck und der deutsche Protestantismus*, Gütersloh, 1994.

I. The Concept of Peace in the Hebrew Bible

1. In the Pre-Exilic Period

a. The Genesis generation, the acquisition of land and the colonization of Canaan

As stated in the Bible story, the exodus from Egypt and the forty-year migration through the desert marked the beginning of a gradual uniting of the different tribes of Israel into one nation. This was all depicted through the revelation of the God of the patriarchs Abraham, Isaac, and Jacob at Sinai, as described by the Pentateuch in Exodus[1].

In the historico-critical retrospective the foundation for the creation of a nation was laid through the entire nation's commitment to monotheism and the establishment of a uniform set of laws given by God to this nation through its leader, Moses.[2]

The struggle of the nation in search of a confined territory in which to settle, which is the most important condition for sovereignty, was presented by later Jewish-Israelite thought to have received divine sanction on the basis of the fusion of religious and national thought, as was common at that time.

The warring environment almost inevitably had to have an influence on the image of God. The term *"Adonai Zebaoth"* (Lord of hosts)[3] clearly shows this. The hosts of God did not originally mean the heavenly hosts, i.e., the cherubs and ser-

---

1. Ex 24.15 ff.

2. See Deut 33.4.

3. The tetragrammaton YHWH, which is interpreted by the critical Bible sciences as "Yahwe" is indeterminable as regards pronunciation. The Jewish tradition, therefore, uses *"Adonai"* for the name of God, which simply means "Lord."

aphs, but rather autonomous war demons[4] who later became subjects of the War God Adonai Zebaoth and, therefore, took their place on Israel's battle lines, the *"ma'arkhoth Israel."*[5]

According to the understanding of ancient Israel, there was a close relationship between God and his people[6], a covenant with heaven which Israel could maintain through the fulfillment of the divine Commandments.[7] It is important in this context that the Ark of the Covenant, which held the tablets on which the Ten Commandments were written[8], symbolizing the bond between God and his people, represented Israel's battle banner, both during the period of the desert migration[9] as well as during battles in the time of Canaan.[10]

This *Adonai Zebaoth* is not only an impetuous "God of Israel's battle lines" who, "powerful in the struggle, makes his sword drunk with the blood of the slain,"[11] as he is portrayed by national elements. Rather, he is also presented as a God of true peace, justice and mutual obligation.

The Book of Genesis is especially important in this regard. Peace is of outstanding significance for the patriarchs. Abraham only waged war once, in order to free his nephew Lot from the hands of the enemy[12]. Isaac and Jacob also lived in peace and worked toward reconciliation with their neighbors. Isaac did not defend himself against the Philistines when they disputed his rights to his water holes, even though a nomad and his flocks needed these wells for survival.[13] Jacob even cursed his sons, Simeon and Levi, because they attacked the Shechemites,[14] even though their sister Dinah had been raped by the son of one of their rulers.

---

4. Their name "Zebaoth" comes from "those going to war."

5. Fritz Bammel, *Die Religionen der Welt und der Friede auf Erden — eine religionsphänomenologische Studie*, Munich, 1957, p. 20.

6. Deut 14.2.

7. Ex 18.23.

8. See Ex 32.

9. Num 10.35.

10. 1 Sam 4.3f. See Bammel 1957, p. 42.

11. Deut 32.41f. See also Deut 20.1.

12. Gen 14.

13. Gen 26.18—22.

Simeon and Levi are brothers; weapons of violence are their swords. O my soul, come not into their council; O my spirit, be not joined to their company; for in their anger they slay men, and in their wantonness they hamstring oxen. Cursed be their anger, for it is fierce, and their wrath, for it is cruel! I will divide them in Jacob and scatter them in Israel.[15]

Jacob's words reflect the disposition toward peace of the God-fearing men in the second millennium B.C.E. This peaceableness and willingness to compromise could be further demonstrated through numerous other examples.

Let us return to the period of land acquisition in Canaan. As an isthmus between Assyria and Egypt, Canaan had always been a center of conflict, a bone of contention among the surrounding nomadic tribes and the many different peoples who populated the area throughout that time period. This unsettled situation and the resulting weakness of the tribes there made it relatively easy for Israel's army, under the protection of their War God *Adonai Zebaoth,* to conquer the area little by little, even though the Book of Joshua reports of difficulties.

Although various biblical testimonials show that the Israelites were expressly commanded not to tolerate any other native religions in Canaan,[16] these religions appear to have indeed had an influence. The city gods seemed to have been either repressed or else certain aspects were incorporated to some extent into the image of a single God.

The Bible describes, for example, the conquest of the Jebusite city-state Jerusalem,[17] the future capital of Israel, which would later become the site of the Temple.

---

14. Gen 34.30.

15. Gen 49.5—7. See J.H. Hertz, *Pentateuch and Haftorahs,* London, 1981, p. 129 (commentary) and Kaufmann Kohler, *Der Segen Jacobs mit besonderer Berücksichtigung der alten Versionen und des Midrasch,* Berlin, 1867, p. 34ff.

16. Num 33.51 ff. Deut 12.2—3, 29—31; 13.7—17; 17.2—5; 9—14.

17. For a general discussion on the problems concerning the relation of Joshua and Judges see Georg Fohrer, *Das Alte Testament,* part 1 (3rd printing), Gütersloh, 1980, pp. 61—63; Josh 10 is not a historical report since we know from the Bible that King David took Jerusalem from the Jebusites.

Looking at it from the angle of biblical studies the Jebusite city-god *"Shalem"* from pre-Israelite times might very well have influenced the image of the God *Adonai* as presented in the biblical texts. This seems especially likely when one considers that, much later, not only the concept but even the name can still be recognized in the Hebrew term for peace, *"shalom."*[18] And the connection between the roots of the words "Jerusalem," *"Shalem,"* and *"shalom"* is obvious. For the further examination of the Israelite concept of peace, it is, therefore, important to outline briefly the duties of the God *Shalem.*

According to Odil Hannes Steck, *Shalem* was responsible for an intact general social welfare, especially within the state of Jerusalem. In addition, his Jebusite followers expected both fertility, and aid to rescue them from enemy threats[19]. Although the Israelites were the only monotheistic people at the time, there were nevertheless very striking similarities between their image of God and that of the Jebusites. The Israelites also expected welfare from God, *expressis verbis* through his promise of a land of milk and honey[20], and protection from enemies. Fertility also played quite an important role for a people involved in the transition from a nomadic to a settled way of life.

It is a central biblical promise that God would give his people fertile land, when and if they declared their intention to observe the Commandments.[21] The image of fertility and peace often appears, even much later, when Isaiah says:

> For thus says the Lord: "Behold, I will extend prosperity to her [Jerusalem] like a river, and the wealth of the nations like an overflowing stream; and you shall suck, you shall be carried upon her hip, and dandled upon her knees."[22]

18. For religious lyric on Jerusalem see Ps 85; as an example of the writings of the prophets see Is 60.17.
19. Odil Hannes Steck, *Friedensvorstellungen im alten Jerusalem*, Zürich, 1972, p. 26.
20. Num 13.27.
21. Deut 11.8—17, etc.
22. Is 66.12; see also Is 48.18, Ps 72.3.

This point represents a junction regarding the ancient Israelite concept of peace. The connection of old traditions of a peaceable life,[23] as demonstrated in the Book of Genesis, with a newly won consciousness in the Promised Land, leads directly to the term *shalom*. The desire for peace grows almost automatically with the acquisition of land of one's own, in order to live and work the land undisturbed and in peace.[24]

Even though the role of power on the basis of arms still remained significant, especially during the many disputes with the surrounding peoples, the longing for peace continued to grow. More and more, peace was considered the ideal through which God's blessings achieve perfection.[25]

This demands necessary changes in the image of God, from whom the gift of peace was expected. Longing for peace picks up on the nomadic lifestyle of earlier centuries and continues its peace-loving tradition. If this had not been the case, the stories of Genesis would probably not have been maintained as they exist today.

The term *shalom* provides the basis for such consideration. A definition of the term offers insight into the conceptions of ancient Israel. *Shalom* includes an all-around, comprehensive sense of welfare, facilitating and supporting life. Benjamin Davidson in his Analytical and Chaldee Lexicon describes the basic meaning of *shalom* as "wholeness," "integrity," "perfection," "well-being."[26] This broad definition is especially evident in Leviticus[27] which in my opinion contains a major part of what comprises the ancient Israelite concept of peace. For example, it says in Leviticus 26 verses 1 and 3: "If you observe my Commandments . . . I will give peace in the land . . ." Good conduct and abiding by the law before God, therefore, serves a peace-keeping function

---

23. See Ps 4.9.

24. Deut 12.10.

25. See Priestly Blessing, Num 6.26.

26. *Encyclopedia Judaica*, Vol. 13, Jerusalem, 1991, Col. 194; cf. Benjamin Davidson, *The Analytical and Chaldee Lexicon*, London, 1970, p. 720f.

27. Lev 26, esp. 3—7.

which, however, can be disturbed by misconduct. *Shalom* represents a blessing for the keeping of the law, but it is embedded in a more comprehensive state of peace, one that includes nature and the animal world.

Essential elements of the Jebusite, or rather, the old oriental concept of peace in general, appear here. Hans Heinrich Schmid summarizes them in three concepts: overflowing fertility, living in safety, and security against the enemy and wild animals.[28]

Odil Hannes Steck can define four areas to which the term *shalom* pertains. First, the *social* sphere: the wish for life-protecting, life-supporting rights that guarantee the welfare of all social classes.[29] The *political* sphere: the absence of the threat of war and protection from attack are two important components of the hope for peace. This implies peace by controlling the peoples and nations, limiting armed power[30] and restricting the abuse of power.[31] The third area is *nature*: peace is understood as a means of taming chaos, preserving the cosmic, natural sense of the world and making human and animal life possible.[32] *God* stands above these other three spheres as the original source of peace, the guarantor of the ideal conditions the people expect of God.[33] The link between the people and their God, their rituals and worship, must be mentioned at this point, consisting primarily of sacrificial rituals in ancient Israelite times.

In summary, *shalom* can be defined as the welfare and state of completion of all creatures, arising from a divine will for peace, including their peaceful coexistence in a way of life based on God's Commandments.[34]

---

28. Hans Heinrich Schmid, *Salôm, "Frieden" im Alten Orient und im Alten Testament*, Stuttgart, 1971b, p. 58.

29. Steck 1972, p. 29.

30. Ps 46.

31. Ps 2; 37.14—15; 76.12; see Steck 1972, p. 28.

32. Ps 104; Steck 1972, p. 27f.

33. Ps 29.11.

34. Ps 34.15; 37.11; 37.14—15; 37.37—40; H. Fries, *Handbuch theologischer Grundbegriffe*, Vol. 2, Munich, 1970 p. 45.

At the same time, however, the above-mentioned section of Leviticus shows how limited this longed-for sense of peace actually was. Verse 7 clearly demonstrates that the political realization of peace was not to be effected any differently than in the rest of the ancient orient. Accepting peace virtually meant surrender, subjugation, and socage of the conquered. The only alternative was plundering and destruction. In other words, peace was often achieved through acts of war, as in Mesopotamia and Egypt.[35] At that time, the commandment "You shall not kill"[36] did not pertain to war at all. The commandment solely forbid the spilling of blood in one's own state, among one's own people.[37]

In this sense, the Bible unmistakably condemned one type of war, that is, civil war, which involved the bloodshed of one's own people.[38] In general, however, war and killing in war were very much accepted.[39]

Peace in the world meant peace in the Israelite world, just as God was considered the God of Israel. Israel remained the center of the world, especially Zion, the holy mountain, in which the earthly and heavenly realms merge[40] and God's throne is that of the king of the world as well.[41] The city of Jerusalem on this hill is, therefore, the city of God, just as it was the city of *Shalem* earlier.

Reflecting on the above discussion it is evident that the Hexateuch[42] and the later writings, up to the Second Book of Chronicles, usually remained within the general scope of ancient oriental thought. The demand for peace from today's perspective cannot be directly derived from it.

---

35. Deut 20.10—14; Schmid 1971b, p. 103f. Steck 1972, p. 25.

36. Ex 20.13, Deut 5.17.

37. Under the conditions at the time, even this signified considerable progress; Schmid 1971b, p. 61.

38. See Lev 19.17.18; Obad 1.10, Book 60; *The Universal Jewish Encyclopedia*, Vol. 8, New York, 1948, p. 419.

39. See 1 Kings 2.5 with the differentiation between bloodshed in war and in times of peace; Schmid 1971b, p. 61.

40. Ps 48.2.

41. Steck 1972, p. 14f.

42. The Five Books of Moses and the Book of Joshua

Covering the period of the national life of Israel, the
Bible naturally reflects the popular viewpoint of the
contemporary nations which does not differ materially
from that of the most modern nations. Not unlike other
nations of antiquity, the mass of Israel believed that
national security rests in armies and armament. Only
the high-souled prophets proclaimed, "Not by might, nor
by power, but by My spirit, saith the Lord." (Zech 4.6).
But with the destruction of Israel's statehood, this
prophetic ideal became the conviction of the people, so
that from that time on peace may well be regarded as a
constant element in Jewish thought.[43]

Nevertheless, the indispensable foundation for later developments was laid. These developments could only grow
out of the spirit of the Pentateuch, the main foundation of
Jewish theological religious thought.

(Excursus: Peace with the animal world)

In order to facilitate understanding of the developments in
later times, I would like to discuss the most unique and controversial aspect of the Israelite hope for peace, that is, peace
with animals. It will be shown that this represents the epitome of an expectation for ultimate peace.[44]

In the beginning, the relationship between human beings
and animals was well-structured, depicting complete peace.
The Book of Genesis[45] describes how "everything that has
the breath of life" received herbs and greens for nourishment. That means that human beings did not hunt and no
animal devoured another. This age of peace ended with the
Flood, after which the animal world also became a source of
nourishment for human beings.[46] It signified the end of the
primeval state of happiness and the harmony of creation
was followed by division. A new order was sanctioned

---

43. Schmid 1971b, p. 61; See Mordecai M. Kaplan, *Judaism as a
    Civilization — Toward a Reconstruction of American-Jewish Life*,
    Philadelphia, 1981, p. 4.

44. On peace with the animal world, see esp. Heinrich Gross, *Die Idee
    des ewigen und allgemeinen Weltfriedens im Alten Orient und im
    Alten Testament*, Trier, 1956, pp. 83—93.

45. Gen 1.30.

46. Gen 9.3.

through the covenant between God and Noah.[47] The memory of a lost but happy state of peace stayed alive, however, and we can see in Leviticus,[48] that prospects for its return were expressed, though it was made dependent on the keeping of the Commandments.

This describes the concept that through moral action human beings can end the discord between humans and animals which was caused by the sinful corruption of the first human beings.[49] This once real expectation of humanity was transferred in time to an expectation for the Final Days,[50] a process which will be analyzed later in detail, in connection with the issue of the Messiah.

For biblical theology a mechanism becomes apparent: the longing for the primeval state of peace, as described in Genesis, leads to the expectation of its renewal in the present. Because this is not fulfilled, the primeval state becomes a projection of the ideal final state in the future.

Looking at the issue of peace with animals it becomes apparent that the Book of Genesis, with its portrayal of the tradition of pre-Israelite nomadic life, retained its meaning in later stages of Israel's history.

b. Pre-Exilic Prophecy

The eighth century B.C.E. marked the beginning of a period resulting in far-reaching changes in the meaning of God. The increasing affliction of the divided kingdoms by the surrounding nations reached a peak with the destruction of the two states: Israel in 721 B.C.E. and Judah in 586 B.C.E.

The latter date is especially significant to this discussion since the capital of Judah was Jerusalem, the important center of Jewish culture. The devastation of Zion, the destruction of the Temple and city, the end of the kingdom and the deportation of the intellectual and inherited aristocracy to Babylon was an unfathomable catastrophe for the

---

47. Gen 9.9.

48. Lev 26.6 (a key section of the entire study).

49. Gen 6.5f.

50. Is 35.1—10.

people and the religion of Israel. In the two centuries before this the appearance of the prophets was, in addition to the Temple, a decisive factor in the survival of Israelite religion.[51]

These historic events are also reflected by the religious poetry of Jerusalem. Psalms 44, 74, and 79 depict a new point of view. Based on this new experience, God's continuous acts of salvation for Jerusalem and his people become a thing of the past.[52] It is particularly interesting to see the great importance these acts of salvation had in relation to the universal workings of God,[53] always connected with the request for the future restoration of a more joyful state.

A new orientation can also be observed in the pre-exilic prophets. By the time of the appearance of Isaiah in the second half of the eighth century B.C.E., old conceptions of his hometown, Jerusalem, were already questioned by world political processes of which Judah and Israel were part. Although Isaiah, on the basis of his birth and education, was a representative of the Jerusalem conception, his teachings alter it dramatically, also as regards the idea of peace.[54] The pre-exilic prophets present themselves predominantly as the prosecutors, admonishers, and heralds of God's judgment. Israel did not keep the divine Commandments and, therefore, was guilty, deserving not salvation, peace, and welfare, but rescue and repentance, at the very best.[55]

Isaiah does not announce a God of peace for the present, but rather a God who avenges the sins of Israel with the swords of other peoples. His message seems to be: if God's chosen people break the peace, then God sends them strife. Here Isaiah's opinion clearly corresponds to the Jerusalem religious tradition, even if he turns around its message. This expectation for the future is addressed clearly in Chapter 2,

---

51. See Deut 18.16—22 (introduction of the prophets); the text is part of the Deuteronomistic texts which are connected with Josiah's reformation.

52. Steck 1972, p. 50.

53. See the crossing of the sea of reeds, covenant, land acquisition, subjugation of the peoples.

54. Steck 1972, p. 53.

55. Schmid 1971b, p. 63.

2—4,[56] wherein Isaiah prophesies joyful peace for all peoples. Heinrich Gross considers such an expansion to be extremely significant; for the first time, the expectation of peace and salvation does not refer strictly to Israel alone.[57]

God judges among nations (verse 4) and shows the way to his teachings, thereby uniting all of humanity under his banner. The absolute prerequisite is, however, conversion to monotheism and the willingness to moral action. Isaiah addresses not only the people of Israel; he refers to all nations and clearly shows the real meaning of the expression "the chosen people of Israel": the "chosen" people are the mediators between the other peoples of the world and the herald of the monotheistic message, for "out of Zion shall go forth the law, and the word of the Lord from Jerusalem."[58]

Such a unification of peoples leads to the end of strife and grants the world eternal peace. Fritz Bammel emphasizes that God commands this through his only source of power, the power of his word, his "mouth," his "lips," his mind, his "righteousness and his faithfulness."[59] The possibility of settling all strife by peaceful means is offered through God's justice and the willingness of all peoples to moral action[60] and the destruction of all weapons. According to Abraham J. Heschel the trade of war will no longer be taught and will be forgotten completely:

> Passion for war will be subdued by a greater passion: the passion to discover God's ways.[61]

> Into a world fascinated with idolatry, drunk with power, bloated with arrogance, enters Isaiah's word that the swords will be beaten into plowshares, that nations will search, not for gold, power or harlotries, but for God's word.[62]

---

56. See also Is 26.12.

57. Gross 1956, pp. 97—101.

58. Is 2.3.

59. Bammel 1957, p. 154; see Is 11.2.

60. Is 2.3—4.

61. Abraham J. Heschel, *The Prophets*, Philadelphia, 1982, p. 184.

62. Ibid., p. 183.

In this way, Isaiah sees a universal, lasting realm of peace, without violence, but with all-encompassing harmony, expressly including the animal world as well.[63]

This thought regarding the possibility of realizing a worldwide realm of peace was so fascinating that other prophets also considered it. In Micah, for example, there is an almost identical passage, which is expanded with another vision:

> but they shall sit every man under his vine and under his fig tree, and none shall make them afraid; for the mouth of the Lord of hosts has spoken.[64]

Ezekiel[65] also shared this euphoria. In Chapter 34.23—31, he picks up the past and promises — for the time following the Babylonian exile — peace with the animal world, abundant fertility of the fields and trees, safety from enemies that threatened Israel from all sides, and a new King David, who would continue in the tradition of his predecessor and his brilliant reign. In this future salvation, a special covenant of peace would be made with God. This covenant would be drawn up with all other peoples convinced of the power of God,[66] though the time of this covenant is not specified.

Isaiah does not refer only to the blessings of the salvation to come when he expresses thoughts of peace. He demands absolute trust in God[67] and shows that the true path to peace — return to and reflection on God — must be started here and now through one's spirit, in order to reach the Final Days:[68] "In returning and rest you shall be saved; in quietness and in trust shall be your strength."[69] In the face of an impending invasion, Isaiah even discourages resistance. And Samson Raphael Hirsch points out that Jeremiah agrees with this opinion.[70]

---

63. Is 11.6—9; see also 29. 17—21; 32.15ff.

64. Mic 4.1—4.

65. Sixth century B.C.E.

66. Ezek 34.30.

67. Is 7.9: "If you will not believe, surely you shall not be established."

68. See Is 32, esp. 15—18.

69. Is 30.15.

70. Jer 27. 8, 11, 12, 17; 38. 2, 17.

In spite of this longing for peace, as expressed in their writings, the prophets in the pre-exilic period remained adamant. The idea had become intolerable that God's will to grant salvation was greater than Israel's guilt, that is, that no matter what happens, God would only act for his people. This helps us to understand the vehemence with which the so-called "false" prophets were attacked in sermons.[71] The argumentation of this group, which one may refer to as "prophets of good fortune" (*"Heilspropheten,"* to use Hans Heinrich Schmid's expression), is only available through the polemics of their opponents, but it can still be determined that men such as Hananiah spoke out for the belief in the religious conception of the chosen nation based on the idea that God will grant *"shalom,"* even if Israel fails. That is why they predicted a prosperous future for the people, although the difficult political situation at the time promised the opposite.[72]

On the other hand, a contradiction emerged with the canonical prophets[73] who held on to the idea that the actions of the people against God and his will result in strife.[74] In their opinion, *"shalom"* could only exist if the people behaved properly. The absence of peace was, therefore, a clear indication of Israel's failure to obey God's commandments.

Of course, one must ask why the "prophets of the scripture" (*"Schriftpropheten"*) were the only ones included in the Biblical Canon and not the "prophets of good fortune" (*"Heilspropheten"*). The reason might lie in the obvious miscalculation of the latter. The historical fact of the Babylonian exile served as sufficient proof of the falseness of their doctrine, which is why they fell into oblivion.[75]

Pre-exilic prophecy is still based on the tradition of the Jerusalem temple. Nevertheless, it opens up a new, more uni-

---

71. Schmid 1971b, pp. 64 and 68.

72. See Jer 14.13; 23.17; 27.9, 14, 16.

73. Jer 6.14; 8.11; Ezek 13.10, 16.

74. See Hos 2 in reference to idolatry; at the same time there are promises of renewal of the covenant in Hos 2.20.

75. See also Deut 13.2—6.

versal way of thinking, out of which important impulses for the further development of Jewish theology arose.

In any case, it is important to remember that pre-exilic scriptural prophecy in the field of politics by no means focuses on the question of the peace and welfare of humanity, but rather on God's honor:[76] "Where humanity sins against God, so must humanity suffer the consequences."[77]

(Excursus: The Concept of the "Messiah")

As I mentioned earlier, Ezekiel links his expectations of the Day of the Lord with a person who succeeds the reign of King David, thereby establishing the realm of peace on earth. This is a further important element in the expectation of the age of peace. It deserves closer examination, for it does not only appear with regard to Ezekiel. Isaiah also awaited a "sar-shalom," a ruler in peace, who is mentioned in conjunction with David.[78] Similar to the issue of peace with the animal world, the mechanism of "the memory of primeval times being transferred to expectations for the future" can be recognized here.

The prophets apparently did not trust in the power of the ordinary Israelite to fulfill God's Commandments, in order to bring about justice in the world and to achieve salvation.[79] Rather, they expected a person upon whom "the spirit of the Lord shall rest,"[80] and who overcomes common human weaknesses by taking on a leadership position and works to bring about the final condition of peace.[81] In any case, I feel it is worthwhile to trace the roots of this concept.

As shown above, the role of ancient oriental thought in the Israelite image of the world should not be underestimated. In analyzing Isaiah 9.5f., it can be seen that vestiges

---

76. See also Job 25.2.

77. Translated from Schmid 1971b, p. 69f.

78. Is 9.1—6.

79. Heschel 1982, p. 184.

80. Is 11.2.

of ancient oriental enthronement forms, and, therefore, the forms of expression of ancient oriental monarchal ideology, continue to have an influence.[82]

> In its original sense, that which is expressed both in naming and in the acceptance of the ever-lasting *"shalom"* should be transferred to the king through the (magical) effectiveness of both the name and (ritualistic) words.[83]

Ancient Israelite religion, however, denies a magical interpretation of the texts about the status of the king. Nevertheless, magical interpretations were known and accepted as correct by the people, whose form of piousness definitely allowed room for magical elements.[84] The gap between their demands and the political reality was indeed obvious, which is why a shift in the meaning could not be prevented. Formulations about the King's status were no longer based on the present, but shifted to take on the form of expectations for an ideal kingdom in the future, providing the first step toward a sense of awaiting the coming of the Messiah. Isaiah's proclamation refers not only to an ultimate king, in the sense of a Kingdom of God, but also very much to a historical ruler. This ruler is first considered a prince of peace in the same way as any other ancient oriental king,[85] but, independent of this initial status, he is later to become the ideal ruler of the Israelites.

It is not easy to say how soon the prophets of the pre-exilic period envisioned the dawn of this kingdom of peace. The

---

81. See Eugene B. Borowitz, *Reform Judaism Today*, Vol. I, New York, 1978, pp. 85—95; it remains unclear whether this lack of trust in one's fellow human beings can be justified theologically, especially since the concept of a personified Messiah in nineteenth- and twentieth-century Jewish theology continued to give way to the abstract expression "Messianic Age."

82. Schmid 1971b, pp. 73ff.

83. Translated from Hans Heinrich Schmid, *Frieden ohne Illusionen*, Zürich, 1971a, p. 36.

84. See Ludwig Blau, *Das altjüdische Zauberwesen*, Graz, 1974.

85. Ezek 37.25—28; Mic 5.1ff.; Zech 9.9: The donkey was the usual means of transportation for the nobility and the respected class.

fact that the *"sar-shalom"* is related to the earlier ruling dynasties,[86] however, and the closeness both in time and in context of the pre-exilic prophets to the Jerusalem religious tradition leads me to conclude that they did *not* assume that the fulfillment of the prophecies would take place only in the distant future. Psalm 72, in which peace is viewed as a deed of an ideal king, can serve as an illustration. Here, traces of the original reference to the Israelite king(s) still exist.

Awaiting the coming of the Messiah in the near future should not lead to the false conclusion, however, that humanity could look forward to the coming of the prince of peace while remaining completely passive. In addition to the above-mentioned element of conversion to monotheism, the prophets also demand of humanity that the people "attempt the impossible again and again, in order to bring about righteousness, justice, love and peace on earth."[87]

2. The Exile and Post-Exilic Prophecy

The political decline of the Israelite kingdoms and the resulting Babylonian exile represents a visible break with theological thought up to that time.[88] Pre-exilic Israel had traced its existence as a nation and the possession of the land directly back to God's action. According to ancient Israelite understanding, the exodus out of Egypt under the leadership of Moses and the takeover of Canaan were directly attributable to the guiding hand of God.

The historical events of the Exile seemed to make the promise of procreation, benediction, and land ownership superfluous. Led away to a foreign land, with neither a king nor a temple, the people questioned whether God had abandoned his people altogether. This conflict of faith led to the following theological conclusion: Israel's guilt had brought God's punishment onto the people. The call was then made to revert to God in order to receive his grace and be assured a life of peace.

---

86. Is 11.1—10; the awaiting of an offspring of the house of David is also expressed here.

87. Translated from Schmid 1971a, p. 39.

88. Schmid 1971b, pp. 79—90.

A sudden turn of events happened amid this hopeless exilic situation, literally causing euphoria for the entire scope of Jewish intellectual life. The Persian King Cyrus revolted against Media, for whom he had been a vassal up to that point, and started an unparalleled victory march. As a direct result, in 537 B.C.E., the first group of emigrants started returning to the "Promised Land" in order to be able to lead a religiously autonomous life.

With Cyrus' specific support,[89] the rebuilding of the temple in Jerusalem was begun. This favorable sign facilitated fundamentally new systems of thought and faith, which also changed the attitude toward peace. Just as the return to God had been the central concept in pre-exilic times, the new focus became peace. The destruction and exile that had been suffered was considered to be the penalty that Israel had to pay, the judgment of God which had now come to an end.[90]

The Book of Deutero-Isaiah[91] begins with the declaration that Israel's guilt had been wiped out, for "she has received from the Lord's hand double for all her sins."[92] The way was then clear for God's salvation and peace,[93] as had been prophesied. The caesura represented by the exile was considered so significant that the new beginning was consciously associated with the start of nationhood. The exodus from Babylon was judged to be an act of salvation, similar to the exodus from Egypt. For those arriving, the more recent land acquisition was closely related to the original one.[94] With that, God's word was once again trusted,[95] his promises did not lose their constancy throughout the time of the judgment,[96] and God proved himself to be the

---

89. Ezra 1.2—4.

90. Is 48.18; announcement of the return to the homeland through Jer 29.10, 11; 33.6; Ezek 37.25—26.

91. Is 40.1.

92. Is 40.2.

93. Is 45.7; see Ps 128.5, 6.

94. Is 41.17—20; 43.16—21; 49.8—13; 52.4; 55.12f.

95. Zech 4.6.

96. Is 40.21; 41.26ff.; 46.9 ff; 48.5ff., 16.

Almighty One[97] who had renewed his covenant with his people.[98] For this reason, faith in God's promise of peace once again prevailed,[99] and the dawn of salvation seemed near.[100]

The construction of the second Temple sparked a special eschatological hope. The prophets Haggai and Zechariah clearly demonstrated the religious hope that was connected with the reconstruction of the Temple. With the laying of the foundation for this sacred building, the deprivation, want and uncertainty of the beginnings in the homeland dwindled; the Temple marked the start of a new epoch of peace and benediction.[101] The virtues of love of truth and righteousness were reconfirmed.[102] The intensity was felt even more strongly when Haggai[103] spoke of the disruption and shock to the world and its inhabitants who brought their treasures for the decoration of the Temple. In return, God would grant the most precious of all gifts of salvation, complete peace for all.

But all too soon this joyful euphoria was confronted with a serious problem in the face of the already tangible beginning of the eschatological future. Similar to the first Christian community that awaited Jesus' return, it was a persistent problem that the time of salvation did not come. The logical consequence of this experience: the expectation of the Last Judgment was simply pushed into the far future, having no direct relationship to the historical events of the present.

An example of the sobering effect that the reconstruction phase in the post-exilic period had on the Israelites is offered by Psalm 85. According to Psalm 85, the final time of peace has not yet come, but God will still grant peace to the people and his pious followers:

---

97. Is 40.12—18, 21—26; 41.21—29; 43.8—13; 44.6—8.

98. Is 55.3—5.

99. Is 52.6—7; 54.10, 13 f.; 55.12; Ps119.165.

100. Is 52.1—2; Ps 122.6—8. The constant parallels to the exodus from Egypt makes a similar parallel between Moses and the Messiah seem plausible.

101. Zech 8.9—13.

102. Zech 9.16.

103. Hag 2.6—9.

Surely his salvation is at hand for those who fear him,
that glory may dwell in our land. Steadfast love and
faithfulness will meet; righteousness and peace will kiss
each other.[104]

Despite its temporal distance, this time of peace still represented the final goal on the horizon, which seems to shimmer
even brighter, the farther away it is. It was Max Wiener who
pointed this out:

The Messianic realm is not the end of this world, it is
the realization of the moral ideal; it satisfies the divine
Commandments. The prophets know only one world,
the earthly one. It has its place in eternity as the scene
of a humanity which is struggling, erring, and finally,
as a result of satisfying the divine doctrine, united.[105]

In Chapter 60, (Deutero-) Isaiah represents an important
aspect, using images with which we are already familiar to
describe Jerusalem's future brightness. The discussion
seems to come full circle, however, when it returns to the
future might of Israel and the oppression or annihilation of
recalcitrant peoples,[106] just as at the time of the first national period (537 B.C.E.) of euphoria. *"Shalom"* continues to
refer primarily to those who believe in God and, to this
extent, it is universal.[107] God draws up a covenant of peace
with them,[108] but the sacrilegious do not have any peace,[109]
for their actions do not know *"shalom."* [110]

In summary, the prospect of a neutral world peace that
includes everyone is not the central point in the Biblical

---

104. Ps 85.9—10.

105. Translated from Max Wiener, *Die Anschauungen der Propheten von
der Sittlichkeit*, Berlin, 1909, p. 122.

106. Is 60.14—18; 66; Joel 4; Mic 4.11—13.

107. Is 57.19; on the universalism of the prophecy, see Hermann Cohen,
*Liebe und Gerechtigkeit in den Begriffen Gott und Mensch —
Jahrbuch für jüdische Geschichte und Literatur*, Vol. 3, Berlin,
1900, p. 90f.

108. Num 25.12.

109. Is 57.21; 48.22.

110. Is 59.8; cf. Ps 147.10—11.

hope for peace. Rather, the might of God and the assertion of his authority over the world on the basis of arms is significant. *"Adonai Zebaoth"* is presented to be foremost the God of Israel's battle lines in the attempt to preserve the Promised Land for the people of Israel.

Nevertheless, Jebusite influence in the desire for general intact social welfare within Israel's society could be assumed when Israel exchanged its nomadic lifestyle for an existence as settlers and city dwellers. This concern for overflowing fertility and a life in safety and security has unmistakable, important consequences regarding the question of peace, should it indeed be closely tied to the Commandment to live a moral life. The demand for moral action, for "holiness,"[111] and especially the emphasis on the common virtues of justice and righteousness, have a direct relationship to the state of peace or ultimate peace.[112]

We have seen, though, that the political realization of such peace in the greater network around Israel itself showed no difference from the rest of the ancient orient: surrender, subjugation and socage of the conquered. "Peace" meant peace in the Israelite world with Israel's God. Even when principles of good-conduct preserved the peace within Israel, war and killing in war were very much accepted. Prophetic influence with its emphasis on the question of God's honor in the light of the Babylonian exile opened up a new, more universal way of thinking. Inasmuch as the tribal concept of a God of Israel widened into one of monotheistic singularity the path was set for a universal idea of peace among those who keep God's covenant and obey his commandments. In that way the experiences contained in the biblical texts offer the possibility for later generations of faithful of developing a different world view: based on the moral perfection of humanity, an inner pacification was seen to be achievable,[113] which would then be a precondition for peace in general. This pertains especially to ultimate or final peace, which would become evident through a total

---

111. Lev 19.2.
112. Gross 1956, p. 169.
113. Ibid., pp. 148—153.

world harmony based on cease-fire, armistice, and disarmament. Hermann Gunkel went as far as follows:

> Equality among the peoples of the world and, therefore, peace on earth, that is the final notion of the religion of the Old Testament.[114]

In this state of harmony among all individuals and between each human being and God, the divine plan of salvation is completed and all individuals have become perfect beings, "reflections of God," for whom the keeping of the entire moral order is self-evident.[115]

In other words, an order of peace is the ideal of creation, just as awaiting the Last Judgment is the turning point to the original ideal.[116] Such a universal world view might, indeed, be based on biblical roots. To my mind, however, it is a later concept which seeks retrospective validity in the framework of Torah — a common mode of creating continuity in Jewish thought where major breaks occur.[117]

---

114. Trans. from *Die Lehren des Judentums nach den Quellen*, Verband der deutschen Juden, Leipzig, 1923—28, part 3, p. 227.

115. Gross 1956, p. 170.

116. It must be noted that the last judgment does not imply the restoring of paradise (Wiener 1909, p. 118; Hermann Cohen 1900, p. 91). Rather, a profound motif parallel can be seen between both images.

117. Homolka, Walter, *From Essence to Existence — Leo Baeck and Religious Identity: Continuity in Change in Liberal Jewish and Protestant Theology*, Ph.D. thesis, King's College, London, 1992, (U.M.I., Ann Arbor, Michigan, 1993) p. 107f.

II. The Jewish-Hellenistic Symbiosis in the "*Sefarim Chizoniim*," and in Philo and Josephus

Our consideration of the developments following the erection of the second Temple cannot close without taking another area of the literature into account. The *"Sefarim Chizoniim"* [1], were included only in the Greek Septuagintal translation of the Bible, if in any at all. It is extremely difficult to date these writings, though they were generally written from the third century B.C.E. onward,[2] and some even into the Christian era. In order properly to assess the *"Sefarim Chizoniim"* and associated developments, it is important to discuss the significant change which took place in the religious thought of Israel.

(Excursus: The Rise of Individualism)

Since the formation of a nation at Sinai, the people were not so much seen as individuals as they were part of the nation as a whole. The people as a nation had entered the covenant with God. The chosenness by God pertained primarily to the people as a whole and not to individual beings.[3] According to the two stories of creation,[4] which are very significant in terms of evaluating humanity, and according to the portrayal

---

1. "Scriptures not included in the canons of the Bible," i.e., apocrypha and pseudepigrapha.

2. See Leonhard Rost, *Einleitung in die alttestamentlichen Apokryphen und Pseudepigraphen einschließlich der großen Qumran-Handschriften*, Heidelberg, 1971, p. 22.

3. Individuals, such as Moses, play a particular role or satisfy a specific task only as a spokesperson of their community (Gross 1956, p. 93).

4. Gen 1.26 f.; Gen 2.7, 22.

of the life of the patriarchs and their families, it can be said that originally, the possibility of an individual relationship to God did indeed play an important role. The natural desire for such a relationship is also expressed in the Jerusalem religious tradition,[5] as demonstrated in many psalms.[6]

A change was ushered in with Jeremiah, whose prophecy is characterized by a strong individualism[7] that can later also be found in Ezekiel.[8] The Babylonian exile brought with it a break with the tradition of sacrifices in Jerusalem. The connection of the individual to God was then brought to the forefront through the emphasis on prayer as a substitute for the practice of making offerings. At the same time, the prophetic thesis of conversion also includes the principle of living a moral life, something that each one definitely has to do individually, in order to bring about a change in social behavior in the end. This desired change, as I have already described, is directed toward an era of peace — a state of peacefulness in the present as well as the final realm of peace in the future. This future peace is directly tied to conditions in the present — this we can derive from the history of the development of the idea of peace.

1. The *"Sefarim Chizoniim"*

The Apocrypha and the Pseudepigrapha have two important areas of emphasis: the peacekeeping nature of human beings among one another and the establishment of eternal peace. One of the oldest books, "The Wisdom of Jesus Son of Sirach,"[9] clearly criticizes the negative aspects of relationships between individuals that destroy peace:

> Curse the whisperer and deceiver, for he has destroyed many who were at peace.[10]

---

5. Georg Herlitz et. al., *Jüdisches Lexikon*, Berlin, 1927—30, Vol IV, Col. 1168—1173.

6. I.e., Psalms 1, 3, 4, 5, etc.

7. Jer 31.31—34: the new covenant is based in the heart of the individual.

8. Ezek 3.16—21; 18.3—32; 32.1—20.

9. From approx. 190 B.C.E. (Leonhard Rost, *Einleitung in die alttestamentlichen Apokryphen und Pseudepigraphen einschließlich der großen Qumran-Handschriften*, Heidelberg, 1971, p. 50).

10. Sirach 28.13.

Ben Sirach finds pleasure in three things which are "love-
ly before God and humanity":

> agreement between brothers, friendship between neigh-
> bors, and a wife and husband who live in harmony.[11]

For that reason he rejects rage and hatred[12] and praises
God for rewarding the devoted with peace.

> And now bless the God of all, who in every way does
> great things; who exalts our days from birth, and deals
> with us according to his mercy. May he give us gladness
> of heart, and grant that peace may be in our days in
> Israel, as in the days of the old. May he entrust to us
> his mercy! And let him deliver us in our days![13]

The Letter of Aristeas[14] also appeals to the reason of the
individual to be just and to reject violence:

> Moses established a sign that those for whom the legis-
> lation was ordained should practice righteousness in
> their hearts and oppress no one in reliance on their own
> strength nor deprive one of anything, but should guide
> their lives by a righteous rule.
>
> . . . So, by means of such examples the lawgiver has
> taught men of understanding to note that they must be
> just and effect nothing by violence, nor by relying on
> their own strength tyrannize over other people[15]

The idea of justice as a key to peace is also seen in the
exhortation of 1 Enoch,[16] who contrasts the way of death to
the way of peace. In other words, peace is equivalent to life.

> And now I say unto you, my sons, love righteousness
> and walk therein; For the paths of righteousness are

---

11. Sirach 25.1.

12. Sirach 10.6. "Do not be angry with your neighbor for any injury, and
do not attempt anything by acts of insolence."

Sirach 27.30; 28.1 "Anger and wrath, these also are abominations,
and the sinful man will posses them. He that takes vengeance will
suffer vengeance from the Lord, and he will firmly establish his sins."

13. Sirach 50.22—24.

14. From approx. 90 B.C.E. (*Die Lehren des Judentums*, IV, p. 166).

15. Letter of Aristea 147—148 (Henry G. Meecham, *The Oldest Version
of the Bible: Aristeas on Its Traditional Origin. A Study in Early
Apologetic with Translation and Appendices*, London, 1932).

16. From approx. 120 B.C.E. (time of origin discussed in Rost 1971, pp.
103—105).

worthy of acception, But the paths of unrighteousness shall suddenly be destroyed and vanish. And now I say unto the righteous: Walk not in the paths of wickedness, nor on the paths of death, And draw not nigh to them, lest ye be destroyed. But seek and choose for yourselves righteousness and an elect life, And walk in the paths of peace, And ye shall live and prosper.[17]

Purity, the willingness to compromise, nonviolence, justice and the love of truth, in short moral action, is the prerequisite for a peaceful life in the present and it paves the way for eternal peace in the future, a peace which appears transformed, depicted with similar images as in centuries past.

Many nations will come from afar to the name of the Lord, bearing gifts in their hands, gifts for the King of heaven.[18]

And the cities shall be full of good things and the fields rich: neither shall there be any sword throughout the land nor battle din: nor shall the earth be convulsed any more with deep-drawn groans. No war shall there be any more drought throughout the land, no famine nor hail to work havoc on the crops. But there shall be a great peace throughout all the earth, and king shall be friendly with king till the end of the age, and a common law for men throughout all the earth shall the Eternal perfect in the starry heaven for all those things which have been wrought by miserable mortals. For He above is God and there is none else. He too shall burn with fire the race of stubborn men.[19]

---

17. 1 Enoch 94.1, 3—4 (R.H. Charles, translator, *The Book of Enoch*, 7th impression, London 1980).

18. Tobit 13.11 (from approx. 40 B.C.E.; *Die Lehren des Judentums*, IV, p. 166), quoted in Emil Kautzsch et. al., *Die Apokryphen und Pseudepigraphen des Alten Testaments*, Darmstadt, 1975 (4th Edition), Vol. I, p. 146; see also p. 15.

19. Sibyls III, 750—761 (R.H. Charles, ed., *The Apokrypha and Pseudepigrapha of the Old Testament in English*, Oxford, 1913); Sibylline Books: written between 140 and 80 B.C.E., Jewish-based Hellenistic scriptures which had a great influence on Greek thought, especially since the longing for peace that grew in reaction to the 100-year-long Roman revolution (133—31 B.C.E.). This resulted in the hope for a realm of peace and happiness to come, similar to the Golden Age under Kronos (remark the parallel in ideological devel-

And it shall come to pass, when He has brought low
everything that is in the world, And has sat down in
peace for the age of His kingdom, That joy shall then be
revealed, And rest shall appear. And then healing shall
descend in dew, And disease shall withdraw, And anxi-
ety and anguish and lamentation pass from amongst
men, And gladness proceed through the whole earth.
And no one shall again die untimely, Nor shall any
adversity suddenly befall. And judgements, and revilings,
and contentions, and revenges, And blood, and passions,
and envy, and hatred, And whatsoever things are like
these shall go into condemnation when they are removed.
For it is these very things which have filled this world
with evils, And on account of these the life of man has
been greatly troubled. And wild beasts shall come from
the forest and minister unto men, And asps and dragons
shall come forth from their holes to submit themselves to
a little child. And women shall no longer then have pain
when they bear, Nor shall they suffer torment when they
yield the fruit of the womb.[20]

These writings echo themes found in ancient Israel's
prophets, although the "sefarim chizoniim" refer directly to
the situation in paradise, when, for example, peace with the
animal world is referred to. This is even more evident through
the prophecy that labor pains will come to an end, since,

---

opment with history of Israel); Wilhelm Nestle, *Der Friedensgedanke
in der antiken Welt*, Leipzig, 1938, p. 58.

   See also "And then indeed he will raise up his kingdom for all ages
over men, he who once gave a holy law to godly men, to all of whom
He promised to open out the earth and the world, and the portals of
the blessed, and all joys, and everlasting sense and eternal gladness.
And from every land they shall bring frankincense and gifts to the
house of the great God: and there shall be no other house for men
even in future generations to know but only that which he has given
to faithful men to honour. For mortals call that alone (the house) of
the great God. And all the paths of the plain and the sheer banks,
and the lofty mountains and the wild sea waves shall become easy to
travel over by foot or sail in those days. For nought but peace shall
come upon the land of the good: and the prophets of the Mighty God
shall take away the sword. For they are the judges of mortal men
and just kings. Even wealth shall be righteous among men: for this
is the judgement and the rule of the Mighty God." (Sibyls III, 767—
784; Charles 1913).

20. Syrian Baruch-Apocalypse 73.1—5 (from approx. 70 C.E.); ibid.

according to the Bible, these pains first began with the expulsion from paradise.[21]

The authors of the "sefarim chizoniim" go even further than the canonized scriptures. Of course, this might be due to Hellenistic influence, especially in the case of the Sibylline Books.[22] Nonetheless, it is clear how great was the influence of the prophets in subsequent centuries.

2. Philo and Josephus as Representatives of the Jewish-Hellenistic Symbiosis

With Malachi, in approx. 450 B.C.E., the prophetic era came to an end. The subsequent period — up to the war between the Romans and the Jews in 66 C.E. and the final destruction of the Jewish social order in 70 C.E. by Titus — was characterized by political turmoil and intellectual conflict. Aside from internal strife, the Israel of that time was primarily affected by cultural conflicts with the Hellenists and the Romans. Jewish thought was not only restricted to the area settled by the Israelites, however. In all parts of the world known at that time, Jewish communities had long since been established. Through the exchange of ideas, these communities had considerable influence on their neighbors and vice versa. Hellenistic-Roman literature by Jewish authors was very closely tied, both as regards content and the time it was written, to the Apocrypha and the Pseudepigrapha. The Jewish-Hellenist philosopher Philo Judaeus[23] is a prime example.

Philo was concerned with revealing "all that is immortal in us," in order to realize the highest possible degree of peace on earth. The roots of a nonpeaceful existence lie, for him, in the passion of self-interest, without considering justice or injustice. If it were possible to hold this in check, then peace could come to humanity "automatically." All that is good is granted by God's grace, for then the virtue of the humanity "which God loves"[24] would prevail. Human beings, as a reflection of

---

21. Gen 3.16.

22. These are influenced by Hellenism's idea of a "Golden Age."

23. 20 B.C.E. — 54 C.E., from Alexandria.

24. Philonis Opera ed. Coh.-Wendland, 1896: *de optificio mundi I*, 81, p. 28 (Bammel 1957, p. 250).

God,[25] are the crown of creation, but humanity has become so distant from its calling, it no longer resembles God. For Philo, this failure is the reason why humanity is no longer able to reach the state of lasting peace on its own. Through God's teaching,[26] however, humanity is commanded to virtue and peace in order to be prepared, through a peace-serving lifestyle transformed into "justice and love," for eternal peace as a gift of God. What this gift of God looks like can be seen in *"de praemiis et poenis"*:

> [War], which is fought intentionally and which arises out of greed, will easily be eliminated; for humanity, I believe, will feel shame, after escaping the injury and destruction brought on by animals, that they show themselves to be more brutal than these irrational animals. For it will naturally be seen as a great sin when poisonous, human-eating, uncivilized animals turn to peace and reconcile themselves; the naturally tame creation, on the other hand, with an innate social sense, the human being, unreconcilably blood-thirsty toward fellow humans.[27]

Again, the idea of peace with the animal world appears, in this case even serving as an example for humans, originally peaceful, so-called rational beings, to recognize the wrongness of their behavior.

Philo, merely a representative of his time, goes further than the prophets when he views individuals as such and no longer distinguishes between nations. This also corresponds to the emphasis in *"de specialibus legibus I,"* that the Israelite high priest spoke his prayers of thanks and supplication for the entire world and all of nature as well, in total contrast to the priests of other peoples.[28]

---

25. Gen 1.27.

26. Philo, de virtutibus (de caritate), M.II., C.-W. 119; trans. from Die Lehren des Judentums, III, p. 219: "That is primarily what Moses, the devout prophet wishes to achieve through his law: harmony, community, a common ethos and harmonious nature; characteristics, through which families of the cities, nations and lands, the entire human race in fact, can achieve the highest state of blessedness."

27. M.II 423, C.-W. 91/92; trans. from *Die Lehren des Judentums*, III, p. 219

28. Philo: de specialibus legibus I (de monarchia II); M.II 227, c.-W. 97; trans. from *Die Lehren des Judentums*, IV, p. 93: "The priests of other peoples recite the prayers and perform the sacrifices only for

Flavius Josephus, who emphasized the neutrality of God in times of war,[29] also refers to nonviolence in his historical work "The Jewish War":

> Nothing so much damps the force of strokes as bearing them with patience; and the silence of those who are injured diverts the injurious person from afflicting.[30]

This work deals with the turmoil in Israel from the time of the Maccabees (170 B.C.E.) until the fall of the mountain fortress Masada (73 C.E.). Jerusalem had been razed three years earlier by Titus, an event that marks a major turning-point in the history of Judaism, the completion of the transformation from sacrificial worship to a religion of the scriptures, and the increased restructuring of society from that of a nation to that of a religious community.

In spite of the unquestionable Greek, particularly Platonic,[31] influence on Philo, this image of peace is essentially a familiar one. The high demands on humanity which are not fulfilled, the command to return to the ideas of God's teaching in order to achieve peace, that is, a peace that will be fulfilled in the future — this is all based on Israelite prophecy. Especially important, in my opinion, is the universality of Philo's theory. It offers an outstanding example of the openness of Judaism toward its environment at the time — an openness that is also obviously directed at converting pagan cultures.

---

their own members, friends, fellow citizens. The Jewish high priest, on the other hand, says his prayers of thanks and supplication not only for all of humanity, but for all parts of nature: earth, water, air and fire. For he sees the entire world as his homeland, as truly is the case, and it is for the entire world that he prays for the grace of the master, requesting his leniency and goodness for all creation." On Philo's doctrine see also Hans Jonas, *Gnosis und spätantiker Geist*, Part 2.1: *Gotteserkenntnis, Schau und Vollendung bei Philo von Alexandrien*, Göttingen, 1966.

29. Onias prays: "O God, the king of the whole world! Since those that now stand with me are thy people, and those that are besieged are also thy priests, I beseech thee, that thou wilt neither hearken to the prayers of those against these, nor bring to effect what these pray against those." (Josephus, Altertümer 14,2; quoted in *The Universal Jewish Encyclopedia*, p.419).

30. Book 2, Chap. 16, Sect. 4; quoted in: *The Universal Encyclopedia*, p. 419.

31. *Philo-Lexikon — Handbuch des jüdischen Wissens*, Berlin, 1935, p. 558.

In fact, Judaism was indeed a missionary religion during the Hellenist period, and Philo also reported the general acceptance of Jewish thought throughout large parts of the Roman world.[32] The Jewish-Hellenist historiographer, Flavius Josephus[33], gives us an impression in the following:

> That a system of law can distinguish itself from others in such an outstanding manner can be explained by the fact that piousness is not made to be a constitutive part of virtue; rather, other good qualities such as justice, steadfastness, composure and total harmony among the people were seen as expressions of piousness and described as such. For all action, activities and speech represent for us a relationship to piousness to God.[34]

Josephus refers here to the prophetic visions of uniting nations in honor of God, as discussed earlier.

---

32. *De Vita Mosis II*, 5 (David Max Eichhorn, *Conversion to Judaism — A History and Analysis*, New York, 1965, p. 37).

33. 37 — approx. 100 C.E.

34. Josephus vs. Apion II, 16, trans. from *Die Lehren des Judentums*, I, p. 38.

III. Views on Peace in Talmudic Times — Mishnah, Talmud, Midrash

The situation at the end of the Roman-Jewish war seemed hopeless. Werner Keller describes the situation as follows:

> The curtain had fallen — the city was ravaged, Jerusalem destroyed, the Temple collapsed! Most of the inhabitants of the land murdered, or dispersed throughout the world — killed in battle, carried off as prisoners and slaves, fled far away in search of protection and shelter. Judea was desolate and devastated, its cities and villages lay in ruins. Widows and orphans abandoned, the weak, the ill and the injured. Neglected fields, olive trees and vineyards grew wild. Everything was dismal and wretched; what could give one hope?[1]

But the Jewish spirit did not perish, for the Torah scholars, the Pharisees, were able to rebuild an active religious life out of what seemed like nothing. This was only possible because other means of practicing their faith had developed in addition to the Temple itself. The establishment of synagogues can certainly be traced back to the Second Temple period, a time in which similar problems had arisen. Due to the use of prayer as a substitute for offerings and the interpretation of scriptures for studying the will of God, it was possible to maintain a religious consciousness without a Temple.

In the houses of study that were built, above all in Yavneh, oral tradition was collected and passed down; later, efforts were started to maintain the tradition in writing. The *Mishnah* was written in 200 C.E., the *Talmud* almost

---

1. Trans. from Werner Keller, *Und wurden zerstreut unter alle Völker — Die nachbiblische Geschichte des jüdischen Volkes*, Munich/Zurich, 1966, p. 80.

300 years later in a Jerusalem and a Babylonian edition.[2] In addition, there are various *Baraitot*[3] that were not included in the *Mishnah* itself. A further source is the *Midrashim*, a collection of homiletic Bible commentaries that also had been started before the beginning of the Christian era. This included the elaboration of biblical narrative and ethical material, incorporating scholastic methods.[4]

All of these writings of the Talmudic period offer exceptional insight into the Jewish thought of the first centuries of the Christian era, which will now be discussed in reference to the question of peace. A short Talmud tract, "Perek Hashalom," represents an appropriate beginning for such a discussion:

> Peace is great, "for the Lord is peace" (Judg 6.24), and the Messiah, "his name will be called . . . Peace" (Is 9.6) and Israel's name is peace, "for there shall be a sowing of peace" (Zech 8.12).[5]

These lines contain all that is important. God, once the lord of the war demons,[6] receives the name "peace"; he himself *is* peace,[7] which is why a violation of peace is equivalent to an offense against God himself.[8] The section on the

---

2. Mishnah: a collection of teachings and legal decisions which, together with a commentary on it by the Gemara, comprises the Talmud. Particularly the Babylonian Talmud found acceptance and is the basis for detailed studies and interpretations up to the present time. The Babylonian edition is what is referred to as the "Talmud."

3. Passages in the Gemara which are supposedly from 70 to 250 C.E. but did not suceed in entering the Mishnah.

4. For a more detailed introduction to such Jewish literature, see Leo Prijs, *Hauptwerke der hebräischen Literatur*, Munich, 1978, and Günter Stemberger, *Geschichte der jüdischen Literatur — Eine Einführung*, Munich, 1977.

5. *The Universal Jewish Encyclopedia*, p. 419.

6. *"Adonai Zebaoth"*; see chapter I, footnote 3.

7. See Lev Rabbah 9,9 (Nathan Peter Levinson, "Friede, Friede, aber da ist kein Friede," *Allgemeine Jüdische Wochenzeitung*, Vol. 37, No. 18, Düsseldorf, 1982, p. 3); Num Rabbah 11, 18 (Louis J. Newman, *The Talmudic Anthology — Tales and Teachings of the Rabbis*, New York, 1978, p. 314); Shabbat 10b (*The Jewish Encyclopedia*, Vol. 9, New York/London, 1903, p. 566).

8. Keeping Posted, *Choose Life*, Vol. 28, No. 1, New York, 1982.

Messiah refers to an ultimate peace at the time of the Last Judgment. All war will end when this time comes, peace will mark the beginning of the new reign,[9] the age of peace will have already dawned,[10] and weapons will become superfluous "as a candle at the zenith of the sun."[11] Israel will also be called Peace. This means that even in the present, peace must be the greatest goal for everyone. Peace as the epitome of goodness[12] is offered to Israel, so that the world will not be devastated by the sword and wild animals,[13] for the world cannot exist without peace. In fact, according to Rabbi Simeon ben Chalafta, God felt that only peace would be a blessing for Israel,[14] which is why he brings peace between humanity and nature, "between Abraham and the fire, between Isaac and the sacrificial knife, and between Jacob and the angel at Jabbok."[15] The unconditional necessity of peace for Israel is just as obvious, since "the angels in heaven above need peace, although they know neither enmity nor hatred, neither jealousy, resentment nor malice; all the more do mortals on earth need peace."[16] This is why God

9. Lev Rabbah 9,9 (*The Universal Jewish Encyclopedia*, p. 419).

10. "Three days before the advent of the Messiah, Elijah will announce: Peace has come to the world" (Pesikta Rabbati 35; *The Universal Jewish Encyclopedia*, p. 420); see Eduyot 8,7 (*Encyclopaedia Judaica*, Vol. 13, Jerusalem, 1971, p. 197).

11. Shabbat 63a (*The Universal Jewish Encyclopedia*, p. 419).

12. Sifra Bechukotai (Newman 1978, p. 312); Num Rabba 11,16 (*The Universal Jewish Encyclopedia*, p. 419).

13. Perek Hashalom (Newman 1978, p. 312), Num Rabbah 21,1: "Great is peace! The world cannot conduct itself except with peace." (Newman 1978, p. 314).

14. Mishnah, Ukzin III, 12 (*Mischnajot: Die sechs Ordnungen der Mischna*, Basel, 1968 (3rd Edition), Vol. IV, p. 676); an older, respected sage is referred to as the younger Joshua ben Levi here, just so that the Mishnah could close with a word of peace.

15. Shir ha-Shirim Rabbah 3, 20 (Newman 1978, p. 314). All events mentioned here are described in the Book of Genesis. I consider this a direct reference to the original state of peace prior to the period of slavery in Egypt; see Num Rabbah 2: "Consider the great value of peace. Peace was the reward Abraham received for his faith and righteousness. It was all Jacob prayed for." (Joseph S. Kornfeld, *Judaism and International Peace — Popular Studies in Judaism*, Cincinnati, Ohio, n.d., p. 9f.).

16. Lev Rabbah 9,9 (*The Universal Jewish Encyclopedia*, p. 419).

reveals the book of Deuteronomy to his people as the source of the teachings of peace, thereby granting them peace.[17] The scholars' task is, therefore, "to increase peace in the world,"[18] spreading it through their students,[19] for the entire Torah exists only for the sake of peace[20] and all divine Commandments are tied to peace.[21] For this reason, Hillel also advised, ". . . be Thou of the disciples of Aaron, loving peace and pursuing peace (Ps 34.14), (be thou) one who loveth (one's fellow-) creatures and bringeth them nigh to the Torah."[22] The Torah is more significant than priesthood and kingdom, and can be fulfilled by "helping one's neighbor in carrying his yoke, always judging him by giving the benefit of the doubt, showing him truth and leading him to peace."[23]

All of these ideas easily show the immense importance that peace had for the Tannaim[24] and the Amoraim.[25] Along with the virtue of justice, peace is among the terms most often used in Talmudic literature,[26] especially in reference to the ability to make peace in a world yet to be redeemed. This is certainly based to some degree on the demands of the prophets regarding moral behavior, though I believe another aspect plays a significant role, namely, the doctrine of immortality or God's judgment.

---

17. Perek Ha-shalom: "Great is peace, for when Israel said 'All the words which the Lord has spoken we will do' [Ex 24.3], God rejoiced in them, gave them the Law and blessed them with peace." (Ibid., p. 419); see also Kinyan Torah 7 and Pesikta de Rab Kahana 12 (105b).

18. Berachot 64a.

19. Yerushalmi, Berachot 60b: "Rabbi Eleazar said, in the name of Rabbi Chanina: The students of the scholars will spread peace in the world." See Is 54.13.

20. Gittin 59b (*The Jewish Encyclopedia*, p. 566).

21. Lev Rabbah 9,9 (*The Universal Jewish Encyclopedia*, p. 419).

22. Mishnah, Avoth 1.12.

23. Mishnah, Kinyan Torah 6 (trans. from *Mischnajot* 1968, IV, p. 362).

24. Tannaim: refers to the over 250 legal scholars 70—200 C.E., whose teachings comprise the Mishnah.

25. Amoraim: refers to the numerous legal scholars in the third to the fifth centuries; their teachings make up the Babylonian and Jerusalem Talmud.

26. *Encyclopaedia Judaica*, p. 196.

The "belief in the eternal determination for each soul and the individual reward of God"[27] became more meaningful, especially since the time of the Pharisees. Good conduct on the part of each individual on earth became important for God's judgment in the hereafter.[28]

> R. Jacob said: This world is like unto a vestibule before the world to come; prepare thyself in the vestibule, so that thou mayest enter the banquetting-hall.[29]

Peace definitely acquires a special status here.[30]

> The Torah impresses upon us not to chase after a Commandment, but simply to fulfill it when we have the opportunity. In reference to peace, on the other hand, we are advised to pursue it at all costs.[31]

Along the same line, in "Perek Ha-Shalom," the importance of peace is stressed: "Other Commandments of the Torah are left up to our discretion, but the Commandment of peace is made unconditionally..."[32] A precondition to achieving peace, however, is finding peace in oneself: "When individuals have made peace with themselves, they are then in the position to pacify the world."[33] What better way is there to achieve peace than to find a balance with one's environment?

> [O]ne should always strive to be on the best terms with his brethren and his relatives and with all men and even with the heathen in the street, in order that he may be beloved above and well-liked below and be acceptable to his fellow creatures.[34]

---

27. Translated from Herlitz 1930, II, Col. 1122.
28. Through Paul and Origen, the immortality doctrine found a place within Christianity, becoming a central aspect of the faith. In contrast, following numerous modifications, this doctrine lost influence in the Jewish religious philosophy of the Middle Ages and is according to Reform Judaism no longer an indispensible aspect of Jewish faith. See also Borowitz 1978, II, pp. 42—49.
29. Avoth IV, 16.
30. Peah I, 1: "Peacemaking, like charity, profits in both worlds." (*The Jewish Encyclopedia*, p. 566).
31. Num Rabbah 19,27 (Newman 1978, p. 319).
32. *The Universal Jewish Encyclopedia*, p. 419.
33. Num Rabbah 19.27 (Newman 1978, p. 319).
34. Berachot 17a.

"Mipenai-darche-shalom," for the sake of peace, even honor must take on a subordinated position. One Midrash story tells of Rabbi Meir, who allowed a woman to spit in his face in front of his students in order to reestablish peace between herself and her husband. This had been the husband's condition for not separating from her.[35] This story also teaches that such an "insult to one's honor" is not really an insult at all, for even God would sacrifice his honor for the sake of furthering peace among the people.[36] And because of Aaron's peace-making efforts, his death was mourned even more than that of Israel's leader Moses, even though Moses was considered a lover of peace as well.[37] Strife is disapproved of as the cause of all discord,[38] and the self-disciplined individual is considered the real strength as opposed to a violent individual.

> Ben Zoma said: . . . Who is he that is mighty? He who subdues his [evil] inclination, as it is said: He that is slow to anger is better than the mighty; and he that ruleth his spirit than he that taketh a city.[39]

For this reason, a broad range of relations exists between representatives of different houses of learning, in spite of their contrasting opinions.[40] In this context, it is very interesting that Biblical heroes have been reinterpreted in the Talmud as "Heroes of the Houses of Learning."[41] Even weapons such as the sword and the bow, as they appear in the Bible, are recorded as "prayer" or "learning,"[42] to eliminate the vocabulary of war. Rabbi Nathan's words are to be interpreted as follows: "'heroes' always means 'heroes of the Torah studies'."[43]

---

35. Lev Rabbah 9 (Newman 1978, p. 315).

36. Num Rabbah 11.16: "Great is peace! God enjoined his Holy Name to be erased in the water of bitterness in order that there might be reconciliation between man and wife." (Newman 1978, p. 313); Yerushalmi Sota 1.4, 16d (*Encyclopedia Judaica*, p. 197).

37. Avoth de Rabbi Nathan 12; Kallah 3 (Newman 1978, p. 314).

38. Sifre to Nasso 2: "Peace is great, discord hateful." (Ibid., p. 312).

39. Mishnah, Avoth IV, 1; see Avoth V, 11.

40. Tossefta Yebamot 1,3 (Ibid., p. 312).

41. *The Universal Jewish Encyclopedia*, p. 420.

42. Berachot 18 b (Ibid., p. 420).

43. Avoth de Rabbi Nathan 23, 1 (*The Universal Jewish Encyclopedia*, p. 420).

Anger, hate, and contempt[44] are faults that must be fought at all costs. Human beings should be "wise in humility, remembering that a mild response drives away fury and furthers peace,"[45] which each one of us hopes for, for everyone,[46] for "even if nourishment is in abundance, it is worth nothing if there is not peace."[47] For this reason, feeling joy over the suffering of an enemy is considered a serious sin[48] that especially hurts God, since every death signifies the destruction of a part of his creation.[49]

The other side of this is expressed in the rabbinical interpretation of Leviticus 19: "Who saves even one single life is to be regarded as if the entire world had been saved."[50] It comes as no surprise, therefore, that Israel's redemption is to come in the form of peace,[51] and the peace-makers are promised a certain share of the world to come.[52] Even if the Israelites were to practice idolatry while living in a state of peace, God would not punish them and evil could not do them any harm.[53]

---

44. Avoth IV, 3 (*Mischnajot* 1968, IV, p. 345).

45. Berachot 17 (Newman 1978, p. 312).

46. Berachot 17a (*The Jewish Encyclopedia*, p. 566).

47. Sifra Bechukotai 1 (Newman 1978, p. 312; *The Universal Jewish Encyclopedia*, p. 420).

48. Mishnah Avoth IV, 19: "Samuel the Small says: When an enemy falls, do not gloat, and when he transgresses, do not feel joy in your heart; the Eternal could see it and would be displeased and give forth his anger." (trans. from *Mischnajot* 1968, IV, p. 349).

49. Megilla 10b; Sanhedrin 39b (*The Universal Jewish Encyclopedia*, p. 420).

50. Trans. from Levinson 1982, p. 3.

51. Deut Rabbah 5,14 (Newman 1978, p. 313).

52. Taanit 22a: "A Rabbi once met Elijah in a crowded marketplace. 'Master,' he asked, 'who among this throng are most sure of eternal life?' The Prophet, in reply, pointed out two men of homely appearance. The Rabbi accosted them. 'What,' he asked, 'are your special merits?' 'We have none,' they answered, 'unless it be that when people are in trouble we comfort them, and when they quarrel we make them friends again.'" (Ibid., p. 316).

53. Gen Rabbah 38,6 (*The Jewish Encyclopedia*, p. 566); Sifre to Nasso (Num 4.21ff.) 42 (Newman 1978, p. 312).

I have already pointed out the connection between the two expressions "peace" and "justice." According to Jewish thought, the administering of justice is comparable to the act of making peace,[54] since the disagreement between the opposing parties is settled by the legal judgment.[55] This is why Rabbi Simon ben Gamliel[56] views justice and peace, as well as truth, as the pillars upon which the world stands.[57] If the course of justice is perverted, then the sword will come into the world.[58] This negative attitude toward weapons during Talmudic times can be seen in Shabbat 6.4, in which weapons are called "offensive and disgusting." For this reason it was forbidden to carry arms on the Holy Sabbath, consecrated by God.

In addition, the sacrificial altar for God had to be built from unhewn stone, for if iron were to be swung over the stone, it would have been desecrated (see Ex 20.22). This drew much attention, especially in later interpretations; for example, the Mechilta de Rabbi Ishmael (Bachodesh 11; 51) assumes that the altar was created in order to lengthen the days of the people, whereas iron serves to shorten them. Further, the altar makes peace between Israel and its God in Heaven, which is why no iron tool of destruction shall be lifted upon it (Deut 27.5). This was then extended, for if it was not allowed to lift an iron tool upon stone, which can neither see, hear nor speak, how much more did peacemaking people need to be protected from evil (see also Sifre Kedoshim 11.8 and the Rashi Commentary to Ex 20.22).

It is also interesting that King David was barred from building the first Temple, because he had "shed much blood and . . . waged great wars" (1 Chron 22.8; 28.3). His son Solomon was granted permission (see 1 Kings 5.4f.).

54. Zech 8.16; Eccles 3.17.

55. Zacharias Frankel, *Der gerichtliche Beweis nach mosaisch-talmudischem Rechte*, Berlin, 1846, p. 90.

56. Approx. 140 C.E.

57. Mishnah Avoth, I,18 (*Mischnajot* 1968, IV, p. 331); Yerushalmi Taanit IV (August Wünsche, *Der Jerusalemische Talmud in seinen haggadischen Bestandteilen*, Hildesheim, 1967, p. 153).

58. Mishnah Avoth V,7 (Mischnajot 1968, IV, p. 357).

The virtues of truth, justice and peace, which were equivalent according to Rabbi Simeon, were also evaluated in another manner. According to the Talmud, even truth could be sacrificed for the sake of peace,[59] which is sanctioned by God himself.[60]

I believe it has been clearly shown how paramount the idea of peace has become in Jewish thought.[61] The Prophets were thought to have announced nothing else but peace;[62] peace has become the highest goal, both between individuals and among nations. It is remarkable how a time of peace set in the present gained ground over Messianic expectations, especially as the Last Judgment seemed to shift into the far future. At the same time, the individual shifted into the center of the practice of the faith.

(Excursus: Peace in Prayer)

In conclusion here I feel it is necessary to examine more closely the realm of prayer, which originally consisted of spontaneous expressions to God.[63] In Yalcut 67b, the following is said of prayers:[64]

> Prayer is Israel's weapon; it is a weapon, inherited from its fathers, which was never abandoned. Facing the greatest of dangers, the Patriarchs and Moses found refuge in prayer; all the prophets praised prayer as Israel's only weapon. David confronted the powerful weapon-wielding giant, armed only with God's name. The descendants of Esau boasted to Israel of their swords and of the strength they inherited from their father; Israel answered only with the prayer of the fathers.

This quotation is historically incorrect, but it clearly shows — and this is the point here — the attitude at the time

---

59. Yebamot 65 b (*The Jewish Encyplopedia*, p. 566).

60. Yebamot 65: "Great is peace; God even changed truth for its sake." (Newman 1978, p. 312).

61. Sifre 199: "Peace is great; even the dead need peace." (*The Universal Jewish Encyclopedia*, p. 419).

62. Num Rabbah 11.16 (Ibid., p. 419).

63. The oldest surviving prayers are from the time of the Talmud.

64. Trans. from Guiseppe Levi, *Das Buch der jüdischen Weisheit*, Dreieich, 1980 (3ed Edition), p. 268.

toward bloodshed and the use of weapons. We have already discussed one component of the Jewish liturgy, the priestly blessing. From the Pentateuch, it then found a place in the daily morning prayers and was part of the daily ritual in the Temple of Jerusalem.

> The Lord bless you and keep you: The Lord make his face to shine upon you, and be gracious to you: The Lord lift up his countenance upon you, and give you peace.[65]

This blessing ends with the wish for peace; only through peace can total happiness be achieved. Not only the priestly blessing ends with this wish, for "there are no blessings or prayers in the liturgy, the Amidah, the Kaddish . . . nor any grace, which do not end with a prayer for peace,"[66] for without it, all prayers are meaningless.[67] On the other hand, all blessings are found in peace.[68]

The Kaddish, as mentioned above, is one of the most frequently recited prayers, even though I doubt that everyone consciously grasps the message of it. The pleas for peace at the end, which have closed every religious service — and in orthodox congregations, every liturgy as well — since the sixth century[69] read as follows:

> May the fullness of peace and of life descend upon us from the light on high. Peace created in his highest, may peace reign over us, over all of Israel and all of humanity.[70]

There are also prayers against hate and envy[71] and for the confessing of our sins, "in which we let our hands do

---

65. Num 6.24—26.

66. Lev Rabbah 9.9 (*Encyclopedia Judaica*, p. 197); Deut Rabbah 5.14: "Beloved is peace! All blessings end with the blessing of peace." (Newman 1978, p. 314).

67. Num Rabbah 11.16 (*The Universal Jewish Encyclopedia*, p. 419); 11.17 (Newman 1978, p. 314).

68. Lev Rabbah 9.9: "Great is peace, for all blessings are contained therein." (*The Universal Jewish Encyclopedia*, p. 419).

69. Ismar Elbogen, "Der jüdische Gottesdienst in seiner geschichtlichen Entwicklung," Hildesheim, 1967 (7th Edition), p. 94.

70. Trans. from *Der Gottesdienst des Herzens-Israelitisches Gebetbuch*, Nuremburg, 1968, p. 73.

71. E.g. ,Yerushalmi Berachot IV, 2: "May it be your will, Eternal One, my God and the God of my fathers, that our hatred is not lifted

violence,"[72] though a plea for peace is very often mentioned directly. "Their ways are ways of grace and all of their paths are full of peace,"[73] is recited after every Torah reading, in order to remind those who pray of the goal of all Torah doctrine. Following is an old prayer of Rab Safra which, though normally no longer part of the liturgy, is included in the Talmud:

> May it be your will, O Lord our God, to establish peace among the celestial family, and among the earthly family.[74]

The family of nations is referred to here, conveying a concept of idyll and harmony, and reducing the bloody wars of all time to what they really are — useless strife. At the same time, this word also refers to the final situation of the world, in which — according to Jewish faith — an ideal family will reside on the earth. But we do not have to delve so far into the past, for even today there are passages in Jewish prayer books that can be traced back to the (late) Talmudic period. Among these, for example, is the new moon prayer, in which a "life of peace" is prayed for at the beginning of each month; and the eighteenth blessing of the Amidah prayer, which was mentioned above.

> Establish peace, goodness, blessing, graciousness, kindness, and compassion upon us and upon all of Your people Israel. Bless us, our Father, all of us as one, with the light of Your countenance, for with the light of Your countenance You gave us, HASHEM, our God, the Torah of life and a love of kindness, righteousness, blessing, compassion, life, and peace. And may it be good in Your eyes to bless Your people Israel, in every season and in every hour with Your Peace. Blessed are You, HASHEM, Who blesses His people Israel with peace.[75]

---

against our neighbors, nor the hatred of our neighbors against us; nor our envy against our neighbors nor the envy of our neighbors against us! May your teachings fill our homes for all the days of our lives, and may our words find a place before you." (Trans. from Wünsche 1967, p. 16f.).

72. Trans. from Hertz 1927—30, III, p. 254.

73. Trans. from Henry G. Brandt (ed.), *Or Chadash — Gebete für Schabbat, Fest- und Wochentage*, Zürich, 1981, p. 128; see also *Der Gottesdienst des Herzens*, p. 178.

74. Berachot 17a; *The Universal Jewish Encyclopedia*, p. 419.

75. Rabbi Nosson Scherman (trans.),*The Complete ArtScroll Siddur: Weekday, Sabbath, Festival; Nusach Ashkenaz*, 2nd ed., New York,

The "Hashkivenu," which is also included in the Talmud, was passed down from the Midrash:

> Lay us down to sleep, HASHEM our God, in peace,
> raise us erect, our King, to life; and spread over us the
> shelter of Your peace. Set us aright with good counsel
> from before Your Presence, and save us for Your Name's
> sake. Shield us, remove from us foe, plague, sword,
> famine, and woe; and remove spiritual impediment
> from before us and behind us and in the shadow of Your
> wings shelter us — for God Who protects and rescues us
> are You; for God, the Gracious and Compassionate King
> are You. — Safeguard our going and coming — for life
> and for peace from now to eternity. And spread over us
> the shelter of Your peace. Blessed are You, HASHEM,
> Who spreads the shelter of peace upon us, upon all of
> his people Israel and upon Jerusalem.[76]

I believe it has been sufficiently shown that peace is a central theme both in prayers as well as in Talmudic literature. "Every truthful prayer is linked with Jacob's seed; every successful war with that of Esau."[77] The concept of God as a harbinger of peace finally suppressed that of a God of war once and for all.

1987, p. 473; the equivalent for the holy days reads as follows: "Establish peace . . . with Your peace. In the book of life, blessing, and peace, good livelihood, may we be remembered and inscribed before You — we and Your entire people the Family of Israel for a good life and for peace. Blessed are You, HASHEM, Who makes peace."

76. Ibid., pp. 336—337.

77. Gittin 57b (*The Universal Jewish Encyclopedia*, p. 419); see also trans. from Max Grunwald, *Monistische Märchen*, Berlin/Vienna, 1921, p. 155 f.:"Abraham destroys idols. Behind him, the dreadful delusion which demands human blood as a religious sacrifice gradually fades. In Esau-Edom, the 'man of the field who knows the hunt,' that which remains from barbarian primeval times still lives, that which allows the beastly desire in the human soul to run amok with bloodshed. In the hunt as in war, as both are carved from the same stone, that which may only be earned through honest work is taken through might. They wish to harvest what they have not sown. Esau-Edom embodies the morality of the mighty, the privileged, the demonic, the primitive. His spirit spills blood for sport, for pleasure, to cool off national hatred in war. . . Jacob-Israel confronts the aberration of humanity as embodied in Esau-Edom in the form of a 'settled,' civilized people, the humanitarian principle."

I have attempted to describe as comprehensively as possible a linear development of the peace notion from early biblical to prophetic and talmudic times. In any case, there must have been motives allowing these changes to have taken place at all. The simple desire and longing for peace represents, in my opinion, the oldest motivating force that made people project their own wishes onto God, seeing God as the origin of all they considered to be good.[78] This was reflected in the religious literature of the time as well as in the more intimate sphere of prayer.

Indeed, this longing might have been strengthened by the growing repression of Judaism by Christianity, which became the state religion of Rome starting at the end of the fourth century.

The loss of the last vestiges of sovereignty during the Roman-Jewish war without a doubt weakened particularistic tendencies in Jewish theology. Left without its own state, nor even its liberation movement,[79] Judaism was given the chance, notwithstanding the awful events which took place in 70 and 135 C.E., to allow its very individual concept of peace to flourish.

---

78. A similar phenomenon can be seen in the Greek world as well. Irene, the Goddess of peace, initially held a rather modest place in the Greek Pantheon as one of the three Horae, the daughters of Themis. Evidence of worship of her is found rarely and rather late (fifth to fourth century B.C.E.). Around the fourth century B.C.E., however, a shift can be seen whereby peace is valued as something positive (Nestle 1938, p. 57). Also, Virgil, Horace, Ovid, and Propertius abhor war (in face of the Roman civil war) and welcome the *"Pax Romana"* of Augustus as the "Golden Age" (ibid, p. 58).

79. I.e., those who encouraged both revolts against Rome.

IV. Medieval Jewish Philosophy and its Attitude toward Peace

Medieval Jewish philosophy[1] also contributed to the maturation process of the concept of peace, even though the way of thinking did not change considerably from that in Talmudic times.

"Around the tenth century, Europe became the center of Jewish history, and this was true for the next thousand years."[2] Prospering congregations were established in Germany, France and, above all, in Spain, where a prolific exchange of ideas took place between Jews and Moslems up to the expulsion of Jews from Spain in 1492.

The relatively peaceful period of settlement of the Jews in central Europe ended with the Crusades in the eleventh century. These had devastating consequences, starting a period of subjugation that was to last for centuries.

The historical situation clearly shows that any real Jewish influence on international problems was out of the question at that time. The discussion on world peace, therefore, remained an academic issue, limited to the future coming of the Messiah.

1. Here, "philosophy' "does not refer to a system philosophy such as that of Plato or Aristotle. One has to realize, though, that similar developments took place at this time in Islam and then also within Judaism and Christianity, based on a revived interest in "classical" philosophy of ancient Greece.

2. Trans. from Abba Eban, *Dies ist mein Volk — Die Geschichte der Juden*, Munich/Zurich, 1970, p. 137.

1. Messianic Peace

The Gaon of Sura, Saadia ben Josef,[3] considers the lasting wars among nations as evidence of the fact that the prophetic visions of peace on earth could only refer to the Messianic Age.[4] Moses Maimonides[5] also did not expect the establishment of a realm of peace for all of humanity until the coming of the Messiah.[6] Only then

> will there no longer be hunger, war, fanaticism, or strife, for goodness will spread everywhere and joy will be as plentiful as particles of dust; the entire world will be concerned solely with God's wisdom.[7]

David ben Josef Kimchi,[8] a contemporary of Maimonides, said that nations would present their disagreements to the Messiah for judgment. Through the wise and just decisions of the Messiah, there would no longer be war.[9] Waiting for the Messiah also took on a very remarkable status. The more oppressive conditions became for the Jews, the greater their longing for a hasty coming of the Messiah.[10]

---

3. 882—942 C.E.; founder of medieval Jewish philosophy.

4. Emunoth ve-Deoth (Teachings and Attitudes of Faith) 7,10 (Encyclopaedia Judaica, Col. 198).

5. 1135—1204 C.E.; most significant Jewish philosopher of the Middle Ages (Philo-Lexikon, Col. 476).

6. Yad ha Chasaka, Melachim 12.5 (Encyclopaedia Judaica, Col. 198).

7. Trans. from Brandt 1981, p. 4.

8. From Narbonne, 1160—1235 C.E.

9. This is explained through Is 2.4; Kimchi's reference to the Messiah rather than to God is interesting (see The Pre-Exilic Prophecy, chapter I, 1b of this work). This is one more indication of the great significance of the messianic concept in the Middle Ages.

10. This resulted in a large number of models based on Messianic expectation. Following are several examples from the Common Era: Jesus of Nazareth, Theudas of Judea (44 C.E.), the "Egyptian prophet" (50—55 C.E.), Manachem the Zealot, Bar Kochba (132—135 C.E.), Moses of Crete (fifth century), Abu-Isa Ishfahani (seventh century), Serenus (eighth century). During the Crusades, there were many Messianic Movements simultaneously, though generally, very little is known of them; some examples are: David Alroy (1160), Abraham Abulafia (thirteenth century), Asher Lemmlein (1502), David Reubeni, Salomo Molcho, Isaak Luria, Chaim Vital Calabrese (sixteenth Century), Shabbatai Zvi (seventeenth century). These movements were contin-

2. Peace in the Here-and-Now

Of course, rabbinical doctrine in the time of the Talmud continued to have an influence on later Jewish religious philosophy, especially in ethical literature dealing with the meaning of peace at home and in the community.[11] From the Middle Ages, therefore, sermons such as those of Rabbi Eleazar ben Judah ben Kalonymos[12] and his contemporary, Jehudah ben Samuel,[13] sound very familiar:

> Honor your parents, make peace among people, lead them to goodness and fear God.[14]

> Do not speak empty works, neither argue nor mock, do not quarrel with evil ones.[15]

> Do not cause strife among people by giving more to one than another.[16]

> The sole purpose of the Commandments of the teachings of Israel is to maintain love and peace among the people.[17]

Neither is the contempt for weapons as illustrated, for example, in Passover Haggadot of the Middle Ages, a new concept. The "wicked son" or the "simple son" are usually

---

ued through Chassidism and Frankism, as well as in the political goals of Chibbat Zion and Zionism, which is sometimes referred to as "secularized Messianism" (Herlitz 1930, IV, pp. 131—134).

11. See, e.g., Isaac Aboab's "Menorat ha Ma'or," 2.7, 61—65 (Encyclopaedia Judaica, Col. 198).

12. 1160—1230 C.E.; Rabbi in Worms.

13. Died 1217; Rabbi in Regensburg.

14. Trans. from Die Lehren des Judentums, I, p. 163.

15. Trans. from ibid., I, p. 21.

16. Trans. from Sefer ha-chassidim § 897.

17. Trans. from Die Lehren des Judentums, I, p. 20; see also Joseph Albo, Ikkarim I, 25: "It (the Torah) exhorts love of one's neighbor: 'You shall love your neighbor as yourself' (Lev 19.18). It removes hate: 'You shall not hate your brother in your heart' (Lev 19.17) and urges love of strangers."

Yechiel ben Yekutiel of Rome: "Humility calls for accepting unjust suffering without retaliation, controlling one's anger and living in peace with one's neighbors. Such conduct should also be shown in dealings with non-Jews." (trans. from Die Lehren des Judentums, II, p. 190)

portrayed as armed soldiers, the "wise son," on the other hand, as a peace-loving sage.[18]

3. Peace as an Abstract Concept

Various philosophical definitions on the basic essence of peace have been passed down. According to Isaak ben Moses Arama,[19] the popular opinion that peace was merely the opposite of strife, is not sufficient in expressing the concept of peace. Much more, peace is something positive, the essential means of enabling all human beings, in spite of their different temperaments and attitudes, to work together for the public good. To illustrate this, Arama used a pearl necklace as a metaphor: the pearls of individual virtue are dull; only when strung together on a string of peace do they radiate, showing their full beauty. For this reason, "peace" is one of God's names, as God is the one who brings together all of creation.[20]

Joseph Albo[21] defined peace as a harmony of opposites. The ideal should not be the one extreme wherein one gains the upper hand over another, but rather, the harmony between a violent temper and patience, between greed and waste. When harmony reigns in the various parts of the soul, then spiritual peace has been achieved.[22]

Peace is also seen as the ultimate good, which will only be completely achieved in the far future, although some expression of it must already exist in the present. This is expressed through peace of the soul, through ethical action of each individual and as part of a community.

Despite these admonitions and allegories, rabbinical controversies were discussed openly, for the debates "for heaven's sake" seemed constructive[23], serving to determine the truth, thereby sanctioning the struggle against heresy.

---

18. This is also the case today; see"Die Pessach-Haggada — Erzählung von dem Auszuge Israels aus Ägypten an den beiden ersten Pessach-Abenden," trans. into German by W. Heidenheim, Basel, no date.

19. 1420—1493 C.E.

20. Akedat Yithchak 74 (Encyclopaedia Judaica, Col. 198).

21. Died 1495.

22. Sefer ha-Ikkarim 4, 51 (ibid., Col. 198).

23. See also Avoth V, 17.

(Excursus: The Kabbalah and Peace)

One movement that was reproached by many as heresy was that of Jewish mysticism, the Kabbalah. Its major work, the Zohar, appeared at the end of the thirteenth century. The importance of peace is also expressed in this text:

> God is peace, his name is peace and everything is joined together in peace.[24]

The struggle for peace is given a cosmic meaning in the Kabbalah. Human deeds are dependent on whether or not harmony reigns in the realm of Zefirot.[25] The virtuous individual supports heavenly peace between God and his Shechinah.[26]

A concrete connection can be seen in that "Shalom" is the name of Zefirah Yesod.[27] "Peace on earth" is depicted through an erotic symbol — a common form of kabbalistic imagery — as a heavenly union in which Yesod brings the stream of blessings to the earth, the Zefirah Malchut.[28]

We can say that the emphasis on peace, as it already existed in the time of the Talmud, continued consistently throughout medieval Jewish philosophy.

In addition to the expectation of a Messianic Age, which took on particular significance, the idea of an "inner peace," that is, harmony with oneself and with others, became the ultimate goal.[29]

The ethical literature of the Middle Ages considered the fulfillment of the Commandments as the suitable means for achieving this "inner peace." Jewish mysticism started to dissociate itself from this philosophy, thereby paving the way for subsequent developments.

---

24. Assembly of Rabbis of the Reform Synagogues of Great Britain, Forms of Prayer for Jewish Worship, Vol. I, London, 1977 (7th Edition), p. 384.

25. Zefirot (Numbers): Kabbalistic concept of the 10 creating powers or Divine Attributes.

26. Shechinah: godly presence among the people (literally: habitation).

27. Yesod: "foundation".

28. Malchut: "kingdom".

29. This harmony within the Jewish community had already gained importance due to the growing enmity of the Christian environment.

V. The Concept of Peace in the Jewish Enlightenment and Emancipation

The Jewish Middle Ages were long and dark. Not until the second half of the eighteenth century, with Moses Mendelssohn,[1] did a new period dawn for the Jews. Nevertheless, it was to be an arduous road, leading eventually to legal equality in 1871. The Jewish communities stagnated in ghettos, sinking into poverty and awaiting daily new acts of repression by the Church and the State it supported.

In Poland, the Jews never totally recovered from the Chmelnitski pogrom, and when, in 1768, the Cossacks from the Ukraine invaded again, the fates of the communities of Podolia and Wolin (Volyn) were sealed, once and for all.[2]

1. Hasidism

Out of the suffering, however, a new, deep faith emerged that stood in sharp contrast to the tradition of the Talmud. This was Hasidism,[3] based on the beliefs of the Zaddik *(tsadik)*, in opposition to the knowledge of the religion of the common faith and the Talmud-educated rabbi.[4] The starting point concerning the question of peace in Hasidism is per-

---

1. 1729—1786; well-known philosopher, literary critic and aesthetician of the Enlightenment; friend of Lessing, precursor of the emancipation and reform movement (Philo-Lexikon, Col. 453—454).

2. The victims of the invaders were mainly Jews; only 10 percent of the Jewish population survived the pogroms. With the divisions of Poland in 1772, 1793, and 1795, the Jewish communities came under the rule of more restrictive laws than under Polish rule.

3. Founded by Israel ben Eliezer, also called Ba'al Shem Tov, 1699—1760.

4. Walter Homolka, Die frühen Haskala-Bestrebungen in Polen, Neue Jüdische Nachrichten, Vol. 5, No. 27, Munich, 1981.

haps somewhat different than that of Rabbinical Judaism, since the followers of this movement are much closer to the Kabbalah, but Hasidism and Rabbinical Judaism show hardly any difference in their statements regarding peace. The Hasidic estimation of the place of the individual shows its concept of peace.

> Each living being . . . owes its life to three creators:
> father, mother and God. And God's portion of the
> human being takes precedence.[5]

This opinion of Rabbi Menachem-Mendel of Kozk clearly shows the demands placed on each individual follower: "who does not stand, remains lying; who does not better oneself, worsens oneself."[6] The human being who has been given life through God constantly has to work to purify himself, since God speaks through the individual,[7] and since the individual, throughout his entire life, leaves traces "in the world above."[8] Good conduct and morality are, then, also binding goals in Hasidism, and serenity and harmony are desirable ideals.[9]

An almost naive love of God and of life are two important characteristics of Hasidic faith, just as the Torah was given to the people in praise of life.[10] A very essential factor in religious experience is community. Only through community

---

5. Trans. from Elie Wiesel, Chassidische Feier, Vienna, 1974, p. 219.

6. Rabbi Aaron of Karlin (trans. from ibid.).

7. Rabbi Menachem-Mendel of Vitebsk: "The individual is the language of God" (trans. from ibid.).

8. Trans. from Martin Buber, Des Baal-Schem-Tow Unterweisung im Umgang mit Gott, Cologne, 1970: "The individual should be aware that he is a ladder, standing on the ground with the top reaching heaven, and all his movement and action and speech leave traces in the world above."

9. Trans. from ibid.: "The individual is to be moved only by God. If he is stirred by an evil love, he must direct his love to God alone and all his efforts are directed to God. And if he gets angry, and it is an evil fear which derives from violence, then he must violate this urge and build a wagon of it for God."

10. Rabbi Abraham Kalisker: "The entire world is full of treasures; no one has the right to despise them. What did I learn in Mesritsch? Simply that the Torah was given to the people in praise of life and of all things which make life worth living." (trans. from Wiesel 1974)

can the individual grow beyond himself and touch the "heavenly throne."[11]

In other words, individual acts, to some extent, represent the extension of the arm of God on earth, and all individuals must behave accordingly. This "accordingly" refers to the peaceful conception of God from prophetic, or rather, Talmudic times. Human beings have been placed on the earth to live, doing so according to God's will. In the end, the will of God will break violence, for "the word can silence the gun."[12] Based on this approach to life, it is obvious why Hasidim strictly object to performing military service, as was the case with most Jews in the eighteenth century.[13] Conflicts with religious opponents, however, were indeed fought with physical means. Nachman of Braslav, a Hasidic leader who was controversial throughout his lifetime, even taught that only the Zaddik could lead his followers to true service for God, since the Zaddik has enemies and, therefore, something to fight for.[14] It comes as no surprise, therefore, that Rabbi Leib, the "Grandfather of Spola" prayed:

Redeem your people, Lord, before it is too late.
Otherwise you run the risk of not having anyone left to redeem.[15]

Unfortunately, his words had to be referred more urgently to the threatening situation of the Jews in their Christian surroundings than to internal conflicts among the Jews.

2. The "Wissenschaft des Judentums"

While Hasidism was developing in Eastern Europe, the Age of the Enlightenment was dawning for western Judaism. Its

11. The Maggid of Koshnitz: "One who wishes to grow beyond oneself can only achieve this through others, with their help and by helping them. If all the children of Israel would hold out their hands to each other, then they could build a chain and touch the heavenly throne." (trans. from ibid., p. 123).

12. Rabbi Nachman of Braslav (trans. from ibid., p. 168)

13. See for example, Simon Dubnow, Weltgeschichte des Jüdischen Volkes, Jerusalem, 1971 (2nd Edition),Vol. III, p. 25, 268f.

14. Encyclopaedia Judaica, Col. 199.

15. Trans. from Wiesel 1974, p. 51.

most outstanding representative was the philosopher Moses Mendelssohn. He gave the impulse essential to leading Judaism out of the ghetto it was forced into during the Middle Ages. Consequently, a struggle for emancipation began, bringing a certain amount of acculturation with it. With the French Revolution of 1789—91, Jews became citizens with equal rights for the first time within a European state. In Germany this status was not granted until 1871, with the founding of the Prussian Empire.[16]

This social opening also had considerable consequences for the religion. The twofold nature of the "Jewish question" in the nineteenth century is marked by emancipation and anti-Semitism.[17] The emancipatory period started at the end of the eighteenth century and continued up to a judicial act of emancipation, the law of the North German Confederation of 1869.

The background leading up to this is to be found in the Enlightenment — period: in its secularization process and, most importantly, in the transformation of society from feudalism to modern bourgeois capitalism.

In the liberal consciousness of the Enlightenment, emancipation was seen as a kind of collective educational process of Judaism, based on the dissolution of the Jewish group identity and, with that, of the confessional status of the Jewish religion (De-Judaization).

The Jewish acceptance of this emancipation took place in a dynamic process of adaptation to the structures of the develop-

---

16. With that, the desire to perform military service became a symbol of this bourgeois equality — a futile hope for real equality, in retrospect; see also Rolf Vogel, Ein Stück von uns — Deutsche Juden in deutschen Armeen 1813 — 1976, Mainz, 1977.

17. See Reinhard Rürup, "Emanzipation und Krise: Zur Geschichte der 'Judenfrage' in Deutschland vor 1890," in Juden im Wilhelminischen Deutschland 1890—1914: Ein Sammelband, Werner E. Mosse and Arnold Paucker (eds.), Schriftenreihe wissenschaftlicher Abhandlungen des Leo Baeck Institut 33, Tübingen, 1976, pp. 1—56; and Reinhard Rürup, "Die 'Judenfrage' der bürgerlichen Gesellschaft und die Entstehung des modernen Antisemitismus," in Reinhard Rürup, Emanzipation und Antisemitismus: Studien zur 'Judenfrage' der bürgerlichen Gesellschaft, Kritische Studien zur Geschichtswissenschaft 15, Göttingen, 1975) pp. 74—94; for a general overview, see further: Jacob Katz, Zur Assimilation und Emanzipation der Juden, Darmstadt, 1982 and Walter Homolka, From Essence to Existence, p. 43—51.

ing modern society. This was characterized by the increasing
number of mixed marriages and conversion to Christianity, as
well as by a growing indifference of Jews to their own religion.[18] In the hope of accelerating the emancipation process,
Jews demonstrated primarily liberally-oriented politics.[19]

Here I am not so much referring to the tendency toward
christening that took place at that time, though the effects
of this movement were indeed drastic. Rather, within
Jewish theology itself, the nineteenth century marked a
time of vehement debate, resulting in a division of Judaism
into several denominations.[20] Above all, I would like to discuss the developments in Germany, where these differences
were most pronounced. The group that represented the origin of such differentiation was the "Wissenschaft des
Judentums," ("Science of Judaism"), an expression first
used by Leopold Zunz in 1823. The goal of this group was to
conduct systematic, critical, scientific research, in contrast
to the one-sided, dogmatic, dialectic teaching methods of the
Middle Ages. Leopold Zunz's book, Die gottesdienstlichen
Vorträge der Juden historisch entwickelt,[21] was published

18. See G. Mai, "Sozialgeschichtliche Bedingungen von Judentum und
    Antisemitismus im Kaiserreich," p. 121, in T. Klein, V. Losemann, G.
    Mai (Eds.), Judentum und Antisemitismus von der Antike bis zur
    Gegenwart, prepared for the Department of History of the Philipps-
    Universität Marburg, Düsseldorf, 1984, pp. 113—136; and Monika
    Richarz (ed.), Jüdisches Leben in Deutschland, Publication of the
    Leo Baeck Institute, 3 vols, Stuttgart, 1976/78/82; Here: Vol. 2:
    Selbstzeugnisse zur Sozialgeschichte im Kaiserreich, Stuttgart,
    1978, p. 16.

19. See Jacob Toury, Die politischen Orientierungen der Juden in
    Deutschland: Von Jena bis Weimar, Schriftenreihe wissenschaftlich-
    er Abhandlungen des Leo Baeck Instituts 15, Tübingen, 1966.

20. Old Orthodoxy, Neo-orthodoxy, Hasidism, Liberalism or Reform
    Judaism, Conservatism, and in the twentieth century, the newest
    branch, Reconstructionism.

21. See Caesar Seligmann, Geschichte der jüdischen Reformbewegung
    von Mendelssohn bis zur Gegenwart, Frankfurt a.M., 1922, p. 88; on
    the entire development, see Friedrich W. Niewöhner, "Judentum.
    Wesen des Judentums," in: J. Ritter and K. Gründer (Eds.),
    Historisches Wörterbuch der Philosophie, 4, Darmstadt, 1976, pp.
    653—658; and Heinz M. Graupe, Die Entstehung des modernen
    Judentums: Geistesgeschichte der deutschen Juden 1650—1942,
    Hamburger Beiträge zur Geschichte der Juden 1, Hamburg, 1969.

in 1832, marking what is considered the birth of the "Science of Judaism" and scholarly reform of Judaism. By giving evidence for an evolutionary process in the history of Judaism, Zunz gave scientific grounds for Reform ideology.[22]

Zunz inspired the first generation of Liberal Rabbis, of whom Abraham Geiger (1810-1874) was the leading representative.[23] In their conceptions of this evolution, Jewish tradition, which had been considered as a unified whole up to that point, was divided into a persevering "core" and its changing temporal manifestations; i.e., the fundamental elements of the "essence" were defined.[24]

This process of historicization was accelerated through emancipation and assimilation. The validity claims regarding apparently obsolete aspects of Jewish tradition were dispensed of by Jews through consistent historicization. A science of Judaism that was emancipated and disassociated from theology was to aid the integration into the developing modern society.[25]

---

22. See Gösta Lindeskog, Die Jesusfrage im neuzeitlichen Judentum. Ein Beitrag zur Geschichte der Leben-Jesu-Forschung, With an epilogue to the reprint, Darmstadt, 1973 (Uppsala, 1938), p. 41.

23. See Yehuda T. Radday, The Unity of Isaiah in the Light of Statistical Liguistics, Hildesheim, 1973, p. 189: "he emphasizes the universalism of Judaism that through the destruction of the Jewish state and the spreading of the diaspora broke through"; (Yehuda Radday in reference to Abraham Geiger's Lectures on Judaism and History from 1865 to 1871, see Abraham Geiger, Das Judenthum und seine Geschichte, Breslau, 1865 (2nd Edition).

24. See Bernhard Isaak, Der Religionsliberalismus im deutschen Judentum, (unpublished doctoral dissertation, University of Leipzig, 1933), p. 48f.

25. See Kurt Wilhelm, Wissenschaft des Judentums im deutschen Sprachbereich: Ein Querschnitt, Schriftenreihe wissenschaftlicher Abhandlungen des Leo Baeck Instituts 16, 2 Vols., Tübingen, 1967, here: Vol. 1, p. 3f.; and Lindeskog 1973 (1938), p. 40f.

See also the negative comments of Leo Baeck to the resulting development: "Das Judentum wurde ein historisches . . .," see Leo Baeck, "Theologie und Geschichte," in Leo Baeck, Aus drei Jahrtausenden: Wissenschaftliche Untersuchungen und Abhandlungen zur Geschichte des jüdischen Glaubens, with an introduction by H. Liebeschütz, Tübingen, 1958, p. 33; see also his positive appraisal of Troeltsch in this context: Ibid., pp. 30—32.

On the emergence of the "Science of Judaism" from Historism, see Hans Liebeschütz, Das Judentum im deutschen Geschichtsbild von Hegel bis Max Weber, Tübingen, 1967, pp. 113—156.

As early as 1836, Geiger called for the founding of a Jewish theological faculty representing this new approach; in 1854, the first Jewish Theological Seminary was established in Breslau, and in 1872, the "Lehranstalt für die Wissenschaft des Judentums," an institution of higher education for the science of Judaism, was founded in Berlin. The growing controversy, in which assimilation was regarded as an insertion into a Christian-dominated culture, resulted in a return to specific aspects of Jewish tradition.

In this context, I would like to introduce two philosophers who dedicated their work to the tradition of the "Wissenschaft des Judentums."

a. Moritz Lazarus (1824—1903)

Moritz Lazarus was a professor of philosophy in Bern and Berlin. He was an influential leader in German Judaism in the second half of the nineteenth century, especially within liberal circles. Lazarus was a co-founder of the Hochschule für die Wissenschaft des Judentums (Advanced Academy for the Scientific Study of Judaism) in Berlin and was a spokesperson of moderate religious liberalism, advocating respect for Jewish tradition and humanitarianism.

Tolerance and openness were important prerequisites for the realization of Jewish ideals, according to Lazarus.[26] While "paving the way of peace," which is "one of the highest goals of a moral lifestyle," national restrictions need to be overcome. Peace and patriotism are not mutually exclusive; rather, peace is the completion of the process.

> Popular patriotism is based on the precondition of opposition, conflict, competition among nations (not to mention domination, prestige, exploitation of trade, etc!). The Messianic concept of peace teaches that nations must work together, just as the cities and provinces within a state. To be truly patriotic means: to make one's own state into an effective link in the community of humanity.[27]

---

26. Moritz Lazarus, Die Ethik des Judenthums, 2 vols., Frankfurt/Main, 1904/1911, Vol. I, p. 178ff.

27. Trans. from ibid., II, p. 365.

Moral community must become universal. The claim that "the entire Torah exists solely for the morals of peace"[28] obviously expresses the thought that all ethical legislation flows into the blissful hope of creating peace among all of humanity.

> All cultural acts indeed lead to a uniting of the people and to an exchange and interaction of powers and accomplishments; at the same time, however, there is growth in the national ego. This is where a competitive zeal comes from, which leads to rivalry and struggle. Morality, on the other hand, requires peace — a healthy, beneficial peace. The conflict between mutual accomplishment and individual selfishness must be resolved.[29]

It is the task of moral teachings to determine the justifiable limits of both self-centeredness and devotion. Peace as a spiritual and ethical ideal means neither destruction nor exploitation of the weak, but rather the maintenance, support, strengthening and development of relative perfection in the weak. The true meaning of peace is, first of all, peace among all of humanity. This does not mean peace as a transaction with someone in particular, but peace as a fundamental way of thinking that is the basis for all interactions. By this, Lazarus means a uniting of all of humanity in moral action that will necessarily bring about a general state of peace. By finding a compromise between the individual ego and the common welfare of all, the final Messianic Age is brought closer. Lazarus does not allow any choice; because God obliges human beings to moral conduct, they must bow to God's wishes.

It is important to note that Lazarus' contribution to the Jewish concept of peace may be seen in the reawakening of universalism, which had been losing influence since the time of the Talmud as a result of external factors. In the nineteenth century, Jews considered themselves to be citizens who were obliged to introduce their sense of ethics into world affairs.[30] Their unrelenting insistence on the concept

---

28. Trans. from Gittin 59b.

29. Trans. from Lazarus 1904/1911, II, p. 342 ff.

30. H. Steinthal, On Jews and Judaism: "Did not the doctrine of eternal world peace go forth from Zion, in which the nations would live with and among each other as brothers? Judaism is international, just as humanitarianism is; international Jewry must integrate itself into

of peace in face of times of increased nationalism and violent wars is especially remarkable in this regard.[31]

b. Hermann Cohen (1842—1918)

Hermann Cohen, professor at the university in Marburg, was the most outstanding representative of the Neo-Kantian Marburg School. He based his theories concerning ethics on Jewish moral teaching, consciously developing it further. During the final years of his life, Cohen held lectures on general and Jewish philosophy at the Hochschule for the Wissenschaft des Judentums, which was co-founded by Moritz Lazarus in Berlin. Cohen also saw peace as the major factor in harmonizing all of morality and as the quintessence of all divine attributes.[32]

> Divine peace is God's perfection, his face, the ultimate archetype of human morality.

God is peace, God represents harmony of the moral powers of the world with their natural conditions, for Cohen God is a God of love of humanity, and God demands such a love of humanity from those formed in his image. Accordingly, peace becomes a symbol of human perfection, individual harmony and the perfection of humanity. For peace does not merely depict the absence of war. It is a symbol of the Messianic Age, a positive image, the epitome of morality.[33]

Not until the time of peace is the process of human spiritual salvation completed, according to Cohen. Through peace

---

the prevailing international relations." (trans. from Die Lehren des Judentums, III, p. 223).

31. See also Morris Joseph, Judaism as a Creed of Life, London,1903, pp.452—455: "The Jew who is true to himself will labour with especial energy in the cause of peace; he will strive to bring about the change of temper in men, that juster attitude towards the question of War and Peace, which alone will permanently put an end to international strife. Never can he consistently belong to a war party. His religion, his history, his mission, all pledge him to a policy of peace, as a citizen as well as an individual." p. 454; Encyclopaedia Judaica, Col. 199.

32. Trans. from Hermann Cohen, Religion der Vernunft aus den Quellen des Judentums, Wiesbaden, 1978, pp. 515—533.

33. Cf. Arama's view in the Middle Ages (chapter IV, 3 of this work).

as the common power of human consciousness, all forms of love will be freed from ambiguity. Only in peace can the individual be freed of selfishness and be able to experience true love.

> The prophets taught of this trust in world peace as the goal and purpose of the history of the world. With these thoughts, they prove themselves to be the true teachers of compassion. For war is the Satan of world history. It is also a mockery of the thoughts of God, the father of all humanity, just as it contradicts the concept of humanity as an end in itself or the ultimate aim, that one may think as did the ancient Greeks, that war is the father of the universe; that one may think that the real meaning of life and of human fate is found in war.[34]

Peace, which is the goal of the moral world, is much more the primeval power in that world. The highest goal, namely, the fulfillment of peace, is achieved by means of self-perfection and peace of the soul. This peace of the soul is expressed in a sense of satisfaction that makes one independent of the striving for exaggerated material needs, therefore paving the way for further study. It is not mere faith without understanding that provides the basis for peace of the soul,[35] rather, this peace is based on reason.

All passion, in contrast to peace of the soul, has its source in hatred. The religious doctrine of virtue must fight against hatred, since it is based on love.[36] Peace, however, forms the path of virtue, not only to avoid hatred, but to exclude and prevent it.[37] In order to eliminate hate, Cohen tackles the issue of loving one's enemies.[38] There is never a reason to hate, which is why one can love one's enemies, thereby fulfilling the Commandment to love one's neighbors.[39] Only when one knows no enemies at all is it possible to remove hate from one's heart.

---

34. Trans. from Hermann Cohen, Innere Beziehungen der Kantischen Philosophie zum Judentum, 28th Annual Report of the Lehranstalt für die Wissenschaft des Judentums, Berlin, 1910, p. 58.
35. In contrast to Hasidism.
36. Love of God and humanity.
37. Hermann Cohen 1978, p. 520f.
38. Hermann Cohen 1900.
39. Hermann Cohen 1978, p. 521f.

All hatred is futile, I deny hatred in the heart of
humanity. For that reason, I deny that I have an enemy,
that a person could hate me.[40]

By eliminating hate from the inventory of powers of the
soul, the long awaited peace of the soul finally approaches.
Tranquillity and contentment can now be achieved. For a
personal sense of peace, however, belief that national hatred
has been eliminated from human consciousness is also necessary. When hate is recognized as an illusion, this becomes
possible. Just as humanity will be able to imagine the virtue
of peace, they will be able to unmask the deadly image of
hate. All doubt and disturbances of the peace are obstacles to
the inner life, misinterpretations and afflicted aberrations.[41]
Peace is most certainly the basic power of the human soul,
just as it is the goal of humanity. Peace is, therefore, in
everything and over everything. And just as the Hebrew root
of *"shalom"* means "perfection," it is also the purpose and the
goal of humanity, which is striving toward perfection.[42]

> Peace uses all other purposes of nature and the intellect
> as its own means. . . . Peace as the purpose of humanity
> is the Messiah who will free humanity and all nations
> of conflict, mediating this strife among individuals and
> bringing about the reconciliation of the people with
> their God.[43]

The meaning and value of life lies in peace.

> It is the unity of all powers of life, their balance and the
> resolution of all their differences. Peace is the crown of
> life.[44]

Peace is the path which, even if by way of death, leads to
eternal life.[45] For Cohen as well, morality represents the
basic principle and highest aim of humanity. With this he
addresses the individual and, at the same time, the entire
world. Just as God is peace, the human being also signifies

---

40. Trans. from ibid., p. 522.
41. Ibid., p. 524f.
42. Ibid., p. 529.
43. Trans. from ibid., p. 529.
44. Trans.. from ibid., p. 531.
45. Ibid., pp. 531—534.

peace. The concept of harmony, according to Cohen, is indispensable. And the way to achieve peace is also shown, namely, by means of self-perfection through religious study and peace of the soul. When hatred is removed from the world along with the word "enemy," then peace will come in the form of the Messiah[46] who will reconcile the people with their God.

Up to now, loving one's enemies had not been expressly mentioned, even though the Commandment to love one's neighbor leads in this direction, and morality condemns hatred, vengeance, and gloating. Cohen places particular significance in the love of one's enemies, however, and with that, introduces an important new element into thoughts on peace. Cohen is strict and uncompromising in his argumentation when he refers to peace as the epitome of the meaning of life. He might have learned this relentlessness from World War I, which he experienced in the last years of his life.

In my opinion, Cohen's teachings represent the completion of the transition that Judaism had been experiencing for several centuries. This transition led from the worshipping of the "Adonai Zebaoth" in the original sense of the word to that of an absolute God of peace, an image which actually has more in common with the thought of that generation which created the Book of Genesis. To some extent, he returns to an original way of thinking, which he considers to be natural as compared to historical wisdom.[47] Cohen tries to build a bridge to modern times on the basis of philosophical thought.

Hermann Cohen marks the end of the Jewish Enlightenment. His theories, which were consistent up to the end, offer an outstanding example of idealistic thought, even though the historical facts of his time and the consequences clearly demonstrate the failure of his efforts.[48]

---

46. Thus, the Messiah is no longer seen as the bringer of peace, but as a personification of the situation once peace has been achieved.

47. Ibid., p. 523.

48. Arthur A. Cohen (ed.), Essays from Martin Buber's Journal "Der Jude" 1916—1928, Alabama, 1980, Vol. 3, pp. 33—41.

VI. The Jewish Reformation

The work that was done in the area of the "Wissenschaft des Judentums" influenced Jewish theology, as I have already mentioned briefly. The critical debate on Jewish thought resulted in two major schools within Judaism, namely, Neo-Orthodoxy, led by Rabbi Samson Raphael Hirsch,[1] and Reform Judaism, whose most radical leader was Rabbi Abraham Geiger.[2]

While Hirsch held on to traditional practices, Geiger and his supporters introduced the Jewish reformation. Its goal was the further development of Jewish theology according

---

1. 1815—1889; trans. from Brandt 1981, p. 3: "The greatest goal, hallowed by Judaism, is that all people be free, that they recognize and accept God, and that they use their intellectual and material powers freely and generously in the service of truth and justice on earth, providing for both the smallest hut and the most luxurious palace. For this reason, nothing should be considered Jewish which hinders Jews from using all their powers toward this goal. They must not simply idly watch the happenings of the modern age, they must participate with all their heart and soul, for it is a divine Commandment that love and justice be achieved on earth. This is why God brought Abraham from the opposite shore of the river and chose him and his descendents to benefit the world through their deeds and their suffering."

2. 1810—1874; trans. from Geiger 1865, I, p. 138: "In the inspiring proclamations which the prophets of Judaism, filled with absolute trust, delivered to the world, that there would come a time when only the one God would be recognized and accepted, when total peace would surround and bless humanity, in this view of a noble future of truth and friendship among all peoples, there was a definitive power which granted Judaism duration and courage, and there was an indefatigable self-confidence which went hand in hand with the development of humanity. In face of the legend of ancient Greece through which the Golden Age, the cradle of humanity, began, while the times became more and more worthless, Judaism retained the high belief that humanity is the fertile ground upon which the spiritual seed should ripen. This is the reason for such powerful perseverence within Judaism; this hope has proven itself to be the holding power, lasting over the centuries."

to modern needs.[3] The connection between the emancipatory "Jewish question" and the emergence of a bourgeois capitalist society was, at the same time, the necessary condition for the anti-Semitic turn of events that took place during the stabilization crisis of the Second German Empire. The Catholic stereotyping of the cultural struggle as a "war of Judaism against Christianity," the defeat of the Liberals in the election of 1878/79 and Bismarck's antiliberal turnaround intensified this process.[4]

In this sense, modern, racist anti-Semitism was a postemancipatory phenomenon that represented the ideological bond of the "antagonistic nationalism"[5] of the Empire, therefore acquiring the quality of a world view.[6] The situation at the turn of the century was greatly influenced by the "Berlin Anti-Semitism Debate," which was triggered by Heinrich von Treitschke in 1879, based on the speeches

---

3. On the history and works of Reform Judaism, see W. Gunther Plaut, The Rise of Reform Judaism: The Growth of Reform Judaism, New York, 1963/1966 and: Sylvan D. Schwartzman, Reform Judaism Then and Now, New York, 1971.

4. However, Bismarck was not seen from a Jewish perspective as being anti-Semitic out of conviction; anti-Semitism was merely a political tool of incitement for him; see "Bismarck posthumus," Allgemeine Zeitung des Judentums: Ein unparteiisches Organ für alles jüdische Interesse. (Founded by Rabbi Dr. L. Phillipson; Ed.: Dr. G. Karpeles; after 1909, L. Geiger; Leipzig/Berlin, 1870ff.) 63 (1899), Nr. 15 of 14 Apr, pp. 169—171.

5. Hans-Ulrich Wehler, Das Deutsche Kaiserreich 1871—1918, Deutsche Geschichte 9, 4th Edition (reviewed and with expanded bibliography), Göttingen, 1980 (1973), p. 108.

6. See Reinhard Rürup, Emanzipation und Antisemitismus: Studien zur'Judenfrage' der bürgerlichen Gesellschaft, Göttingen, 1975, p. 91.

On the history of the term "anti-Semitism" see P. Nipperday/ Reinhard Rürup, "Antisemitismus," in Geschichtliche Grundbegriffe: Historisches Lexikon zur politisch-sozialen Sprache, Otto Brunner, Werner Conze and Reinhart Koselleck (eds.), Vol. 1, Stuttgart, 1972, pp. 129—153. Quoted in the reprint, Rürup 1975a, pp. 95—114.

Rürup 1975a, p. 74, clearly differentiates between modern anti-Semitism and pre-bourgeois, religiously motivated enmity toward Jews; for another view, see Uriel Tal, Christians and Jews in Germany: Religion, Politics and Ideology in the Second Reich, 1870—1914, (translated from Hebrew by N.J. Jacobs), Ithaca, N.Y./ London, 1975 (Jerusalem, 1969), p. 305.

leading up to the debate by Adolf Stoecker, one of the court chaplains at the time.[7]

Theodor Mommsen, supporter of the liberal resistance to Treitschke, recognized very early that this debate made anti-Semitism socially acceptable. The reins of shame ("Kappzaum der Scham")[8] were loosened, no longer holding the movement in check; the debate became an issue of academia.[9] As early as 1890, prominent liberals such as Mommsen, H. Rickert, and others founded the "Verein zur Abwehr des Antisemitismus," an organization to fight anti-Semitism. The most prominent member representing a theological perspective was Otto Baumgarten. Soon after, in 1893, German Jews formed their own association, the "Centralverein deutscher Staatsbürger jüdischen Glaubens."[10]

Around the turn of the century, anti-Semitism was by no means an explicit social movement, but a hidden, anti-Semitic tendency definitely existed in society.[11] The Jewish attitude at this time was ambivalent. Some retained the old dream of total assimilation[12] while others, most notably the

7. See the important bibliography: Der Berliner Antisemitismusstreit (Quellensammlung), Walter Boehlich (ed.), (Frankfurt a.M., 1965). On Treitschke, see Hans Liebeschütz, Das Judentum im deutschen Geschichtsbild: Von Hegel bis Max Weber, Schriftenreihe wissenschaftlicher Abhandlungen des Leo Baeck Instituts 17, Tübingen, 1967, pp. 157—191.

8. Theodor Mommsen, Auch ein Wort über unsere Juden, Berlin, 1880, p. 11.

9. See Norbert Kampe, "Akademisierung der Juden und Beginn eines studentischen Antisemitismus," in Wolfgang Dreßen (ed.), Jüdisches Leben, Berliner Topografien 4, Museumspädagogischer Dienst Berlin — Ästhetik und Kommunikation, Berlin, 1985, pp. 10—23.

10. See Arnold Paucker, "Zur Problematik einer jüdischen Abwehrstrategie in der deutschen Gesellschaft," in Werner E. Mosse (ed.), Juden im Wilhelminischen Deutschland, Schriftenreihe wissenschaftlicher Abhandlungen des Leo-Baeck-Instituts 33, Tübingen, 1976, pp. 479—548.

11. For the Jewish perception of anti-Semitism around the turn of the century, see M. Phillipson, "Jahresüberblicke," in JJGL (Jahrbuch für jüdische Geschichte und Literatur), Verband der Vereine für jüdische Geschichte und Literatur in Deutschland (ed.), Berlin 1889ff., and Gustav Karpeles, in AZdJ 1898ff.

12. See Richarz 1978, 2, for an eloquent example.

Zionists, had already abandoned the concept of assimilation.[13] It became more and more obvious that, for the sheer sake of preserving Judaism, "assimilation" was only desirable if a distinctive Jewish group identity could be maintained. That is, Jewish tradition needed to be reformulated in such a way as to be compatible with the conditions of modern society and culture.

The historical significance of "liberal" and also of "conservative" Judaism, from the very beginning and especially at the turn of the century, is determined by their involvement in this task.

(Excursus: Samson Raphael Hirsch, 1815—1889)

Before turning to the movement of Reform Judaism, it is useful to examine the concept of peace in the thinking of Samson Raphael Hirsch as a representative of neo-Orthodoxy. Hirsch's main statements embodying his conception of peace can be found in an exegesis to Psalm 72,7:

> "Shalom" encompasses more than just social peace
> between human beings — rather, it is the harmonious
> concord of all conditions, circumstances and relations.[14]

"Peace" for Hirsch does not merely denote political and social peace in the narrower sense. It is more comprehensive and inclusive, referring to the entire web of relations in the world. Its characteristic feature is a state of harmony, of balance — both in the individual and his surrounding network of relations and circumstances.

The creator and grantor of this peace is God. He alone is in a position to accept the repentance of the human being forgetful of his responsibilities, and to restore him to a state of harmony with himself, his environment and God.[15] The

---

13. On the relationship of the "Centralverein" to the Zionist Movement, see Jehuda Reinharz, Fatherland or Promised Land: The Dilemma of the German Jew 1893—1914, (Ann Arbor, MI 1975), esp. the summary (pp. 225—234) and the extensive bibliography (pp. 290—312).

14. Samson Raphael Hirsch, Die Psalmen, Frankfurt am Main, 1924, Pt. I, p. 331f.

15. Samson Raphael Hirsch, Israels Gebete, Frankfurt am Main, 1921, p. 161.

path God has laid out for man in order to arrive at "peace,"
that state of inner and external harmony, is God's teaching,
the religious Law.[16] A person who leads a life pleasing to
God becomes a catalyst for peaceful and harmonious social
existence:

> "Ish shalom" [i.e., a "man of peace"] is the total opposite
> of . . . "risha" [an "evildoer"]: not only is his life never a
> disruptive breach or offensive caprice; it is far more,
> bringing "complement and perfection" everywhere, fur-
> thering the "salvation" of all beings which come into
> contact with him.[17]

The concepts of "peace" and "harmony" in Hirsch's work must
always be conceived in relation to their referential source,
namely "God" and "man." God creates peace, and is its con-
solidator; without his blessing, a God-fearing person cannot
experience the joyous feeling of peaceful harmony.[18] However, it is man who brings peace into the world, thus becoming an exemplar of God's blessing and teaching.

In summary, Hirsch's concept of peace can be viewed as a
logically consistent expression of his Orthodox religious outlook and philosophy of life. God's blessing and law are the
key determinants of the condition of "peace" in the world. It
is man's task to bring himself and his environment closer to
a state of blessedness and harmony by following the path of
religious Orthodoxy.

1. Leo Baeck (1873—1956)

Rabbi Leo Baeck was to be the outstanding theologian of
Reform Judaism in the first half of the twentieth century. In
his work, *Das Wesen des Judentums* (*The Essence of Judaism*),
Dr. Baeck[19] was the first to deal systematically with the liberal religious views of the nineteenth century.

16. Hirsch 1924, Pt. II, p. 245.

17. Ibid., Pt. I, p. 189.

18. Hirsch 1921, p. 155f.

19. For a detailed introduction to Leo Baeck, see Albert H. Friedlander,
Leo Baeck: Teacher of Theresienstadt, London, 1973, and Walter
Homolka, "Continuity in Change — Liberal Jewish Theology in a
Christian Society," in: Homolka, Walter and Ziegelmeier, Otto (ed.),
Von Wittenberg nach Memphis, Göttingen, 1989, p. 90—119.

According to Baeck, Jews lack the satisfaction of an observer "who has enough cherished tranquillity,"[20] lack the ancient serenity which opposes their moral will to teach others and to better the world. The optimism of Judaism consists of the hopeful faith in goodness.

> It is faith in God and the resulting faith in humanity; in God, through whom goodness is real, and in humanity, which can realize goodness.[21]

Goodness cannot be known without human beings cherishing a certainty that the future belongs to them. Even the prophets recognized transitory and permanent elements in the lives of the people.

> Everything which serves pure power will pass; the purpose of all violence is to collapse sooner or later. . . . It always destroys itself in the end. Faith in violence is faith in the void and, therefore, it is idolatry. Only that is lasting which God bears witness to, that is, goodness, that which serves right, that which fulfills God's Commandments. . . . There is only one future, that of goodness, that of justice.[22]

For this reason, violence, repression, conflict, and war should disappear from the face of the earth, and humanity will be led only by God's Commandments and justice, bringing all people together to form one humanity.[23] Inner peace and peace with and in God are important prerequisites,[24] as well as the longing that comes from spiritual aspiration and struggle.[25]

A central concept in this context is love of one's neighbors, which expressly includes the loving of one's enemies.[26] Humanity must be recognized in the wicked, and godliness

---

20. Trans. from Leo Baeck, Das Wesen des Judentums, Wiesbaden, n.d., p. 89.

21. Trans. from Ibid., p. 90.

22. Trans. from Die Lehren des Judentums, III, p. 212; see also Martin Buber in a letter to Mahatma Gandhi: (trans.) "Whoever is part of Israel cannot want to practice violence."

23. Ibid., III, p. 213; see Borowitz 1978, III, pp. 97—100.

24. Baeck n.d., p. 158.

25. Ibid., p. 201.

26. Ibid., p. 236.

must be found in the enemies of God. For in the unity of humanity, all people are connected with one another.[27] In order to treat one's enemies justly, one must "love" them, which in this case primarily means "not hate."

> The goal which he (God) gives us is repentance, reconciliation, peace among all of humanity.[28]

The road of all human beings to their future leads to peace via the elimination of hate. This peace is

> nothing sentimental, it is nothing which is released through mere passion. The peace which the prophets spoke of includes a moral task, a Commandment; it shows the path which all individuals should pave and along which they should go.[29]

This striving for peace, however, addresses the community as the sum of all individuals. The human community — and community only exists where love and justice have been achieved — should "fulfill life, creating relationships among the people"[30] which serve to teach them, for community means the special longing for peace. When this longing is finally satisfied and becomes reality, then the eternal will be revealed in humanity, the existence of peace on earth will lead to a reconciliation of the finite with the infinite, immanence with transcendence.[31]

> The goal is . . . to return to the source, return to the pure, to the creative, to oneself; life in the kingdom of God which the individual shall create. . . . That which is good in us, let us see what will come, what the future of humanity will be.[32]

This future describes the concept of a Messiah.

> The Jewish faith in a Messiah requires new individuals who are earnest . . . and this is why the concept of

---

27. Ibid. p. 236.
28. Trans. from Ibid., p. 239.
29. Trans. from Die Lehren des Judentums, III, p. 213.
30. Trans. from Baeck n.d., p. 245.
31. Ibid., p. 257.
32. Trans. from Ibid., p. 257f.

peace also has something driving, pushing, almost rebellious.[33]

For all great thoughts that are thought through to the end, to the time of the Messiah, are a contradiction, a protest against the status quo, which is to be changed actively in order to move toward this peace.[34]

This is my attempt to make sufficiently clear the uncompromising emphasis which Leo Baeck attaches to efforts toward peace. According to Baeck, peace is the only future for humanity, and each and every one of us must find peace in ourselves and in our community.

Lazarus, Cohen, and Baeck are mutually dependent and build upon each other.[35] The issues raised by Lazarus are further developed by Cohen and then made absolute by Baeck. According to Baeck as well as Cohen, love of one's enemies and the elimination of hate represent important steps toward the achievement of peace.

This peace refers back to the past, the source, and it must be worked toward in the present in order to achieve it, finally, in the future. This will in the very end signify the dawning of the kingdom of God.

2. Progressive Judaism Today

Baeck's message has spread throughout the entire world and the heralds of this message have become a model for twentieth century theology. Love of peace has become a key concept in the thinking of all Jewish denominations since the enlightenment age. Neo-Orthodoxy and Conservative Judaism remained loyal to their halachic ideals. It was this background that forced the conservative "Rabbinical

---

33. Trans. from Ibid., p. 280.

34. Ibid., p. 281.

35. It must be emphasized that this collaboration did not take place formally, but rather only in terms of the content of their ideologies; see Hermann Cohen, Jüdische Schriften, Vol. 3, Berlin, 1924: "Das Problem der jüdischen Sittenlehre. Eine Kritik von Lazarus' Ethik des Judentums" (trans.: "The Problem of Jewish Moral Doctrine. A Critique of Lazarus' Ethic of Judaism").

Assembly of America"[36] to issue a statement shortly after Adolf Hitler took power on 3rd May, 1933:

> The world has risked so much for war. Let it risk as much for peace.[37]

Progressive Judaism has also traveled further along the designated path and has remained true to the prophetic primacy of peace. Rabbi John D. Rayner gives an excellent example when he writes in "Judaism for Today," the state-of-the-art book of the Union of Liberal and Progressive Synagogues in the United Kingdom:

> Clearly it is the duty of every Liberal Jew to promote international peace.[38]

This emphasis is clearly expressed in revisions and new editions of numerous prayerbooks.

> We bless the Lord who conquers strife, who removes all hatred and brings harmony to His creation. We praise God we cannot see, who binds together all His creatures with unseen threads of service and of love. We honour the master who has brought us from ways of cruelty and shown us the ways of kindness. We bend low before the majesty which teaches us humility and respect for the smallest things in creation. We glorify the source of peace, for peace is the gate to our perfection, and in perfection is our rest. Lord, open our eyes to the beauty of the world and its goodness. Let us be the servants of Your peace which brings all life together: the love of mother and child, the loyalty of friends, and the companionship of animal and man. . . .[39]

---

36. Conference of Conservative Rabbis of the United States, 3 May 1933.

37. The Universal Jewish Encyclopedia, p. 420.

38. John D. Rayner et. al., Judaism for Today, London, 1978, p. 95.

39. Assembly of Rabbis 1977, p. 17f.: remarkable here is the reference to peace with the animal world; see also Brandt 1981, p. 7.

See also Assembly of Rabbis 1977, p. 81: "Lord, we thank you for your gift of hope, our strength in times of trouble. Beyond the injustice of our time, its cruelty and its wars, we look forward to a world at peace when men deal kindly with each other and no-one is afraid. Every bad deed delays its coming, every good one brings it near. May our lives be Your witness, so that future generations bless us. May the day come, as the prophet taught when 'the sun of righteousness will rise with

The attitude of Liberal Judaism is explicitly shown in the resolutions of the Central Conference of American Rabbis (CCAR), which takes an unmistakable position regarding the force of arms. In 1935, the CCAR, in addition to supporting conscientious objection to military service,[40] discussed the resolution

---

healing in its wings'. Help us to pray for it, to wait for it, to work for it and to be worthy of it. Blessed are You Lord, the hope of Israel. Amen."

Union Prayer Book 1922/24 (Union of American Hebrew Congregations):

"Grant us peace, Thy most precious gift, O Thou eternal source of peace, and enable Israel to be a messenger of peace unto the peoples of the earth. Bless our country that it may ever be a stronghold of peace and the advocate of peace in the councils of nations. . . . Praised be Thou, O Lord, Giver of Peace." (Abraham Cronbach, Encyclopedia Judaica, Col. 199; The Universal Jewish Encyclopedia, p. 421).

Brandt 1981: "May the spirit of brotherly love and mutual understanding remove all fear and all prejudice, and heal all injury. O Lord, let the roar of war be silenced in all corners of the world, so that every man shall sit under his vine and under his fig tree, and none shall make him afraid. . . . O heavenly Father, let your kingdom, the kingdom of truth and peace, spread and let the days come in which you will be recognized as the Lord in all the world. Amen!" (trans., p. 124).

Union of Progressive and Liberal Synagogues, Service of the Heart, London, 1967, p. 282: "May it be Your will that war and bloodshed shall vanish from the earth, and that a great and glorious peace may reign in all the world. Let all who dwell on earth perceive and understand the basic truth, that we have not come into this world for strife and discord, hatred and envy, greed and bloodshed, but that we have come into this world only to know and understand You, who are to be praised for ever. Let Your glory fill our minds and our hearts. Teach us so to use our skills and understanding that through us Your presence may come to dwell on earth, and that Your power and the splendour of Your kingdom may be known to all mankind. Amen."

40. The Universal Jewish Encyclopedia, p. 420: "The Central Conference of American Rabbis recommends to its members that they refuse to support any war in which this country or any country may engage, on the grounds that war is a denial of all for which religion stands"; result of the vote: 91 "yes"; 32 "no"; 31 "yes, with reservations"

Ibid., p. 421: Resolution of 1936: "The Central Conference of American Rabbis reaffirms its conviction that conscientious objection to military service is in accordance with the highest interpretation of Judaism and therefore petitions the Government of the United States to grant to Jewish religious conscientious objectors to war the same exemption from military service as has long been granted to members of the Society of Friends and similar religious organizations."

that this conference declare that henceforth it stand
opposed to all war, and that it recommend to all Jews
that, for the sake of conscience, and in the name of God,
they refuse to participate in the bearing of arms.[41]

War with nuclear weapons, in particular, is strongly condemned.[42] This explains the following from the "Guiding
Principles of Reform Judaism" of the CCAR of 1937:

> Judaism, from the days of the prophets, has proclaimed
> to mankind the ideal of universal peace. The spiritual
> and physical disarmament of all nations has been one of
> its essential teachings. It abhors all violence and relies
> upon moral education, love and sympathy to secure
> human progress. It regards justice as the foundation of
> the well-being of nations and the condition of enduring
> peace. It urges organized international action for disar-
> mament, collective security and world peace.[43]

This attitude and the corresponding demands on all of humanity and on God shows Reform Judaism to be a logical consequence of the theological development through the ages.

It represents the current state of a process that has been
continuing over several millennia and which has still not
come to an end.[44] This process will continue to develop as
long as humanity cherishes the wish and the longing for a
better world.

The poet Saul Chernikowsky[45] expressed this idea for
Judaism as follows:

---

41. Ibid., p. 421.

42. Richard G. Hirsch, Thy Most Precious Gift — Peace in Jewish
Tradition, New York, 1974, p. 50ff; JONAH=Jews Organized for a Nuclear
Arms Halt, Judaism, Peace and Disarmament — Some Collected Views,
Leeds, 1982. Samuel H. Dresner, God, Man and Atomic War, New York,
1966. Louis Jacobs, What Does Judaism Say About . . . ?, Jerusalem, 1973,,
pp. 228—230.

43. Samuel S. Cohon, Judaism and War — Popular Studies in Judaism,
Cincinati, Ohio, p. 26.

44. The newest form of Judaism, Reconstructionism, has also taken up
the traditional postulate of peace, above all, encouraging active work for
peace; see especially Kaplan 1981 and Keeping Posted 1982.

45. 1875—1943.

And I have faith in a future, as far away as it may be, in which one nation will praise another and will go its way in peace.[46]

---

46. Assembly of Rabbis 1977, p. 83.

VII. Jews, Judaism and the Concept of Peace in Our Time

> Cain and Abel stand as symbols and examples of the
> most powerful drives plunging men into hatred, blood-
> shed and war, and ultimately toward self-destruction:
> sexual obsession, material greed, religious fanaticism.[1]

The first six chapters of the present volume carefully guide
the reader to an understanding of the concept of peace in
Jewish literature. The development of the idea of peace
sketched there is not some steep progression from national
particularism to universalism. The old, now outmoded thesis advanced by Wellhausen on Biblical exegesis interpreted
almost every universal expression as evidence attesting to
the late origin of the text.[2]

Today we know that thinking about war and peace devel-
ops along parallel tracks within one and the same period,
and that the existential situation in a given era will tend to
nourish one or the other trajectory of thought. Nonetheless,
it is true that Judaism is firmly rooted in the foundation of
the Hebrew Bible, remaining in constant vital touch with
the Torah and particularly the prophets.

As the People of the Book, often powerless within the various countries in which they lived, the Jews lived more within the Biblical vision of peace in which the disenfranchised
and weak would receive support. Moreover, the dream of the
Messianic Age of Peace, reinforced by the prophetic vision,
remained an urgently desired goal. In the Bible, this messianic future was closely related to the land of promise,

---

1. Trans. from Elie Wiesel, *Adam oder das Geheimnis des Anfangs*,
   Freiburg, 1986, p. 58.

2. Homolka 1992, pp. 62—67.

Israel. With the rebirth of the State of Israel, on the sacred soil of the Promised Land, part of this dream seemed to come true within the past four decades. Biblical paradigma renewed themselves, even though ancient rivalisms also came to life again.

There are some moments in history that run counter to the trends of time; and the "PLO-Israel accord" signed on the White House lawn in Washington on the 13th of September, 1993, can be cited as evidence. It was what Stefan Zweig, in his book *Sternstunden der Menschheit* cites as a moment in the history of civilization when a new opportunity is offered that can and does change history. We are still too close to the events in Washington to evaluate them fully — and fanaticism and stubbornness on either side could undo the progress toward peace that was seen by the world at that moment. Toward the end of this chapter, we must take a closer look at what actually happened, what was written down, and what was left unsaid. At this point, when we look at the Jewish tradition of peace, we can only re-assert the strong yearnings for peace that have been part of the Jewish tradition from the beginning of history; and we can acknowledge that the yearnings within the Arab world must often battle against that special curse of the twentieth century — nationalism — which has crushed some of the finest elements within Islamic thought. It is also a problem within an Israel that finds itself surrounded by antagonists, and which then feels that religious and political leaders cannot be trusted, who talk of peace when there is no peace.

In a time of danger, when citizens' lives and the nation are under constant threat from its neighbors, ancient slogans of war are a more common currency of discourse than Biblical declamations of peace. Yet the latter likewise have their irenic parallel in Israel today. The experience of trauma and dream — the Holocaust and the resurgence of a state in Eretz Israel — are the primal facts of Jewish life in our time. And here we encounter once again the universe of ideas of the ancient prophets, whose interpretation of dreams (e.g., Daniel and King Nebuchadnezzar) leads on to the grand vision of a world of peace. After the existential traumata it has endured in this century, Judaism must now stress the age of messianic peace more emphatically than ever before.

Thus, Margarete Susman believes the task of the prophets is to address those worldly powers who bear responsibility for the future:

> This is a magnificent symbol of the fact that any genuine interpretation of dreams reveals a challenge: a call to us from a new reality of which we are not yet aware, a reality we must watch over and creatively mold. It is precisely this dream-sphere of a reality buried beneath our waking life, deeper and thus more real, calling upon us to act, which is the sphere of truth of the messianic kingdom of peace envisioned by the prophets. . . . In its gospel of peace, Biblical prophecy touches the most profound, passionate and pain-laden dream of the human heart, drawing it forth through all the confusion and darkness of our waking existence up into the light. [3]

Judaism cannot exist devoid of Biblical faith, since without a future there can be no present. Without peace, the State of Israel has no future. And to point up the perplexities of Jewish life in our time, we must also acknowledge that without Israel, Jews today could in truth no longer survive. Yet all this is also bound up with efforts to comprehend the concept of "shalom" in our era.

The past extends in shadow and substance into the present, and as the previous chapter tried to show, not all the lessons of the modern age have as yet been critically digested. There are few today who, like the noted American-Jewish thinker Steven Schwarzschild, still read and draw on the seminal work of Hermann Cohen (1842—1918). Professor Steven Schwarzschild's death left a great void in the American rabbinate. He was a Reform rabbi who still believed in the messiah, who had clear and brilliantly expressed teachings in the field of socialism and peace studies; his impact is visible in this chapter.

Nonetheless, Reform Judaism in the United States remains indebted to those neo-Kantian foundations, and Cohenian rationalism and universalism are still essential elements for contemporary Reform Jewish thinking, although his specific conception of peace has been gradually forgotten over the years.

---

3. Trans. from Margarete Susman, Deutung biblischer Gestalten, Stuttgart, 1955, p. 133f.

The quest for peace, which had deepened within the American rabbinate after World War I, gradually eroded within the Jewish community in America, who were far more aware of what was happening in Germany after 1933 than their neighbors. Nevertheless, there were religious leaders, often linked to socialist thinking and the socialist party itself, who continued to speak out for peace. One of the most outstanding and outspoken proponents of Jewish pacifism was Abraham Cronbach, a professor at the Reform rabbinical college in Cincinnati, Hebrew Union College. He was a curious mixture of saintliness and stubbornness (*"chutzpah"* — Jewish impudence, really); and his uncompromising pacifism made him one of the few Jewish thinkers who attacked the war against Nazi Germany. After the war, Cronbach also officiated at the funeral of the atomic spies Julius and Ethel Rosenberg. His comments aroused criticism on all sides — as much from the Communists as from the rest of the community. In a 1948 publication, in London, he expressed his thoughts about the failure of total commitment to pacifism within world Jewry which *should* be so inclined:

> Since the advent of Hitler, belligerency has characterized the Jews throughout the world. Jewish pacifists have virtually disappeared except for a meagre group . . . the Jewish Peace Fellowship. . . . Those of us who are unequivocally opposed to war cannot but deplore the combative spirit which has seized upon our people. This, in our view, constitutes the gravest of the evils which Hitler has inflicted. Hitler's worst fated victims were not the 6,000,000 Jewish dead but the 10,000,000 Jewish living, not the Jews who fell into his clutches but those who escaped. The direst evil wrought by Hitler lay in that which he did to our souls. He drove peace out of the Jewish mind and put war in its place. He banished love from the Jewish heart and put vindictiveness in its place. It is still impossible to foresee the time when the Jewish people will have recovered from this injury. Though Hitler has been annihilated, the Jewish will to fight still exceeds the Jewish will to understand.[4]

4. Professor Rabbi Dr. A. Cronbach, "World Peace and the Individual Jew." in Bulletin No. 19, The World Union for Progressive Judaism. London, January 1948, p. 12.

Few of us — and I include myself — could go along with this interpretation of history or this analysis of the Jewish soul. Abraham Cronbach had his disciples, in particular Rabbi Stanley Brav (a Reform rabbi in Mississippi) and the Conservative rabbi Isidor Hoffman, on the staff of Columbia University as a student counselor. They were also active members of the Jewish Peace Fellowship, which almost disappeared during World War II. But with the advent of the war in Vietnam and the wave of rising protest against nuclear armament, many new members were recruited to its ranks, men and women who saw pacifism as a genuine logical consequence of Jewish thought. If it remained a tiny group that had little impact in the 1980s and 1990s, this might be related to the perception of the next generation who saw this group more as a club for retired pacifists. The action was elsewhere, in those international organizations (SANE, Campaign for Nuclear Disarmament, etc.) where Jews were well represented. A small pacifist group had also survived in London, where Rabbi Harold Reinhart headed the JPF. For almost all Jews, the war against Hitler was viewed as a struggle for survival, and most believed there was ample justification in defending one's own life — even by force and the means of war if necessary. The German-Jewish philosophers of the prewar decades — Cohen, Moritz Lazarus, Leo Baeck and Martin Buber — had little direct impact on this new current of thinking. Indeed, most of their pupils perished in the concentration camps. But an element of this clarion call for peace remained alive as a spark within American Jewry, associated there with a strong sense of the need for social justice, the most important paradigm of Jewish thought in the twentieth century. One need only look at the Civil Rights struggle, at the march from Selma to Montgomery, for example, where dozens of rabbis marched alongside their comrades. Many of the 100 students I brought from Columbia University to Alabama at that time were Jewish; and one of the great moments of my life was sitting at the roadside, around a tree stump for lunch, in the company of Prof. Abraham Heschel, and Henry Schwarzschild of the Civil Liberties Union, listening to Ralph Bunche and to Martin Luther King, Jr.

Today the link between pacifism and the struggle for social justice is an indispensable ingredient in both Christian and Jewish thought. In an age when the Third World is being plundered and the poor nations of the globe inundated with weapons instead of more meaningful goods, commitment to building a better world entails principled opposition to further massive outlays for armament and the destruction of the environment. Greenpeace, the Campaign for Nuclear Disarmament, and Amnesty International are all groups whose wellsprings are in part religious. Though initiatives here have stemmed largely from the Christian community, many Jewish activists have also joined their ranks. However, it is noteworthy just how much anti-Semitism has also reared its head in these circles, in the guise of "anti-Zionism." Without developing this charge at greater length (left-wing anti-Zionism and anti-Semitism have been explored by competent scholars), I would again draw upon personal experience. After a large anti-war demonstration in Berlin, I went to the "Republikaner Klub" with Prof. Jacob Taubes, who had closely worked with Rudi Dutschke, the key figure of West Germany's students' revolution back in the 1960s. As we entered the club, I noticed a Palestinian-produced anti-Israel film being shown. The comments both during and after the film were deeply anti-Semitic, going far beyond political anti-Zionist judgments, and my gently asked questions evoked deep hostility. Long visits in East Germany also indicated to me that the anti-Israel policies of that state drew as much upon left-wing perceptions as upon the residue left from Nazi times.

While the civil rights movements of the 1960s and 70s in the United States had, in many instances, been founded by Jews, the array of peace groups active in the 1980s and early 90s have increasingly tended to focus on the problem of the Palestinians. On occasion, the State of Israel has even been caricatured as the veritable successor to the Third Reich.

This type of attack is more often part of the political language encountered in Europe. Nevertheless, the reverberations of this type of thinking make themselves felt within the meetings of the United Nations Organization (UNO) — not only within the educational organizations and charitable enterprises, but also through the UNO resolution equating Zionism with racism. Since the break-up of the Soviet Union there have been significant changes; but the volatile climate within the UNO today has made it far more difficult to move toward peace in the many areas of conflict that keep expanding throughout the world. If, nevertheless, I still find it important to look at the German scene, this is based upon my conviction that there is a new development here: this strongest country within the European union has moved toward peace and pacifist thinking in many ways — its refusal to join in the war against Iraq is only one example of many. Yet the absorption of East Germany has also taken many anti-Jewish attitudes into the new political structure, together with an often negative attitude toward Israel.

The "Cain and Abel" motif with which we initiated our meditation on the concept of peace within contemporary Jewish thought stresses the intertwining of the oppressed and the oppressor. In terms of the twentieth century, it is hard to move beyond the reality of Holocaust, which has shaped Jewish fate and thought. And, more than a century and a half ago, Heinrich Heine had commented on German book-burning ("where one burns books, one later burns people") and, in his poem, "To Edom," he reminded himself how in times of darkness Edom's claws had been reddened by Jewish blood — but he ended with the outcry that he was becoming more and more like the persecutor (Und ich werde fast wie Du!). The slow search toward peace in our time cannot be seen in isolation. In a curious way, looking at Germany helps us to understand the Jewish quest for light.

An example of this might be found in the current German scene. In 1992, excesses of xenophobia brought the burning of asylum homes and the murder of non-ethnic Germans into the center of public awareness. Anti-racist demonstrations took place, with hundreds of thousands — representing the vast majority of Germans — demonstrating against the new Fascists. The President of the Federal Republic of Germany, Richard von Weizsäcker, gave the main speech in Berlin, but was verbally and physically attacked by a left-wing audience which equated an attack upon the "established" with a statement against racism. Then, Ignaz Bubis, the Chairman of the Central Council of Jews in Germany, came up to the podium, quieted the demonstrators, and permitted the meeting to continue. Bubis is so popular at this point that he has been mentioned as a possible candidate for the presidency of Germany; but he has been wise enough to refuse this candidacy. The world Jewish community, particularly in America and in Israel, still views Germany with ambivalent feelings; but the quest toward living in amity with the neighbor demands self-examination here. And, in Germany, there is certainly still a strain of anti-Semitism, some of it anti-Zionistic and pro-Palestinian.

I believe this phenomenon is to some extent a kind of psychological defense mechanism, the attempt by a younger German generation, oriented toward Europe, to cast aside the burden of guilt from the Nazi past. Perhaps another factor operative here was an overreaction to public discourse in Germany, based on a weariness with being constantly confronted with the Holocaust.

These extreme accusations leveled against Israel have thus been totally dismissed — especially by Israelis, but also in the Jewish diaspora. In the process of mutual diatribe, the genuine suffering of the Palestinians has been obscured, becoming a political issue that was falsely interpreted by both sides. As I hope to make clear, the concept of peace in Israel is in actuality closely bound up with an awareness of the suffering of the Palestinians. Although the Shamir government was never ready to fully acknowledge such a perspective, the tenor of public discourse has changed since Yitzchak Rabin assumed the reins of leadership. It is now possible, especially within Labor Party circles and to their left, to openly declare that the deep longing among Jewish Israelis for peace must also address the suffering of fellow Arab citizens and recognize the multiple injustices endured by the Palestinians. Such phenomena are also a clear indication that the belief in peace and its possible realization is present not only in theology, ethics and daily social intercourse, but is a salient factor on the level of state politics, public discourse, and the economy as well.

If this were the place for an in-depth discussion, one would have to look at the emergence of the civil rights party

Ratz (and its new linkup with *Mapam*, called *Meretz*) and its role in the present coalition; the mass left-liberal movement, Peace Now, must be mentioned here; and the Jewish-Arab party founded in 1984, the Progressive List for Peace, despite the latter's weak showing in the last election. Jewish pacifism in Israel is manifested in the work of *Yesh Gvul* among the military, whose more radical members refuse to serve in the Occupied Territories. At any given moment, a number are serving a month or two behind bars — their suffering largely unsung in the mainstream Israeli press. Then there is the tiny but still extant Matzpen in its several anti-Zionist factions. One could continue along these lines for some time; but we cannot outline all of the complex factors that make up Israeli politics today. What is important is that some of these factors must be noted in the face of a commonly held misconception that sees Israel as an aggressive warlike state disturbing a peaceable Middle-East. Israel is a nation under siege; and its non-pacifist politics have to be seen in the framework of surviving while surrounded by antagonists who can certainly not be viewed as pursuing peace policy. The fact that there are so many groupings within the Israeli scene which, nevertheless, pursue peace, must be noted with not only approval but also admiration.

One must also look outside the field of politics, in those areas where compassion and concern for fellow human beings are evident in the lives of individuals and small communal organizations. As one example out of many, there is that Socratic gadfly, Abbi Nathan, whose public fight for peace has made him known throughout the world. Almost unknown, there are the "Interns for Peace" (*nitzanei Shalom*) founded by Bruce Cohen and other progressive Rabbis, whose quiet work has had an impact on Israeli life far beyond the limited resources available to that group. The State of Israel's President's Award Book in 1993 presented them with the President's award for Improving Israeli Society:

> The President's Award for Volunteers of 1993 is awarded to the volunteers of INTERNS FOR PEACE for their efforts to make a bridge of brotherhood and friendship

between Jews and Arabs and for their response to one
of the pressing challenges facing Israeli society today.[5]

Walter Homolka has commented on how the interconnected
realm of ethics and the economy has begun to pay increased
attention to the problems of the environment and peace:

> For decades now, the capability of the natural bases for
> life to regenerate themselves has been under excessive
> strain. Yet the maintenance and protection of a livable
> environment remain a prerequisite for proper and fit
> conditions of human existence. Thus, one can note a
> growing preference among the population of the First
> World for dealing with environmental issues.[6]

The fact that a peace initiative can be launched within the
matrix of the economy — and not only in the religious
sphere — indicates just how much can be realized today
beyond the confines of formal religious institutions.

The majority of Jews nowadays in Israel and elsewhere
are secular-minded, and most do not frequent the synagogues. On any given Sabbath afternoon in Israel, there are
far more Jews down at the beach or in the park than in
attendance at religious services. In difficult times, beset by
economic hardship and a working week that allows for only
one full day of rest rather than a two-day weekend, Israelis
look for opportunities for recreation, relaxation, and reflection outside the religious framework of the synagogue, even
during the holidays.

Yet — and here we have to try to better understand the
singular character of the "Old-New Land" (*Altneuland*) that
is Israel — one is far more likely to encounter peace initiatives in the secular arena: on the streets of Tel Aviv rather
than in the rabbinical academies of Jerusalem. Indeed, an
unyielding Jewish Orthodoxy in Israel is engaged today in a
struggle for the land mobilizing the weapons of the Bible.
The belief in God-given borders, a theory of the "just war"
and a new reading of ancient Biblical texts, rooted in the
daily exigencies of existential threat, are being used by

---

5. Intern for Peace reports, Vol. 17, issue 2, p. 4, Summer 1993, Tel Aviv.

6. Trans. from Roche et al., Ethische Geldanlagen — Kapital auf neuen
   Wegen, Frankfurt am Main, 1992, p. 28.

militant Orthodoxy to construct solid walls (and barriers) between Israel and her Arab neighbors.

There is a point, of course, where this presentation becomes less than fair to militant Orthodoxy. *Gush Emunim*, religious parties like *Shas*, and other traditionalist groupings are firmly convinced that they adhere to the vision of peace, and that their political actions are based on the Torah and Divine Revelation, which has given them the sacred soil that they are prepared to defend with their lives. With much sadness, I can only state my own position, totally opposed to them, which finds their actions are no more than reactions to their warlike opponents surrounding the Holy Land. The very fact that there are so many Israelis prepared to "trade land for peace" refutes their attempt to speak for all of Israel.

Shalom as a central concept in Judaism is firmly anchored in Jewish prayer: "O Lord, grant us peace" is recited with deep emotion in every synagogue in Israel and throughout the world. Where there is no peace, the hope for it springs eternal. Few would dispute that Israel desperately needs peace — for sheer survival. The other side could afford to lose many wars — but Israel's first defeat would spell its doom and destruction. For that reason, pacifism is an especially difficult option in a situation where you are constantly being reminded of a stark existential threat: your neighbor wants peace — but only after you have been annihilated. Saddam Hussein launched Scud rockets against Tel Aviv and Haifa even though there was no formal state of war between Iraq and Israel. That circumstance acts to paralyze consciousness, making it far harder to explore and elaborate new conceptions of peace.

After the Scud missile attacks, many Israelis did come to the viewpoint that there was no alternative to peace and compromise. The rigid views of Shamir's government were seen as unrealistic, and his party was dismissed. "Secure borders" were no longer seen in terms of the Golan Heights, and one gave support to peace talks, even though they have been unproductive up to this point.

Yet one should recall a remarkable historical fact: a peace movement, philosophy, and theology of peace had sprung up

in the *yishuv*[7] in Palestine even before the establishment of
the state, articulated by thinkers and activists such as
Martin Buber, Samuel Hugo Bergmann, Ernst (Akiva)
Simon, and Judah Magnes. To a certain extent, they were all
outsiders, not bound to the establishment, and for the most
part not religiously Orthodox. Judah Leib Magnes (1877—
1948) had been a Reform rabbi in the United States, and
became the guiding spirit, chancellor (1925) and later president of the newly created Hebrew University in Jerusalem.
Martin Buber (1878—1965), who also joined the University
staff after 1938, was its most renowned figure of genius. Yet
he was not permitted to teach religion as a subject, since the
traditionalists viewed his heterodox ideas with great suspi-
cion, and was only given a formal appointment as professor
of education with a chair in Social Philosophy in later years.

Ernst Simon (1899—1988) and Hugo Bergmann (1883—
1975) had come from Germany, like so many others from
German-speaking Central Europe (after all, Buber was born
in Vienna, Max Brod was from Prague, etc.) who left a
strong German-Jewish imprint on the evolving Jewish culture of the *yishuv* in mandatory Palestine. In Israel, the concept of a "science of Judaism" ("Wissenschaft des
Judentums") managed to achieve almost all the objectives
envisioned by the founders of the movement at the beginning of the nineteenth century in Germany, and even the
new Hebrew University in Jerusalem was significantly
influenced by this current of thought and scholarship.

Although Gershom Scholem (1897—1982), likewise a
founding member of *Brit Shalom*, had rejected the notion of
a German-Jewish symbiosis, migrating from Berlin to
Palestine in 1923, it remains impossible to comprehend the
course of development taken by the humanistic sciences in
the *yishuv* and later in the State of Israel without considering its powerful roots in the transplanted soil of Central
European, German-speaking Jewry. Scholem, a giant in the
field of Judaistic scholarship, held a professorship for
Jewish mysticism and Kabbala at the Hebrew University
beginning in 1933.

---

7. The Jewish community in Palestine before the establishment of the
   State of Israel.

The concept of *shalom*, a central concern within Judaism over the millennia, was also given manifest expression here, notwithstanding the difficulties generated by the time and the concrete hardships and clashes in mandatory Palestine. The constellation of Jewish thinkers in the *yishuv* was decisively molded by this group of scholars whose origins lay in German-speaking Europe, although it is true that the American-born Judah Leib Magnes played a central role in their midst. Yet even in the case of Magnes, the German element was a factor: soon after his ordination as a Reform rabbi at Hebrew Union College in 1900, he went on to study abroad in Heidelberg and Berlin (1900 — 1903). After a distinguished career as a rabbi and a leading figure in American Jewry, Magnes decided in 1922 to emigrate to Palestine. His contributions to Jewish life both in the United States and the *yishuv* were varied and enormous, though our interest here will focus on his efforts to advance the cause of pacifism.

Magnes' thinking in regard to pacifism evolved slowly, even hesitatingly. In 1905, in the aftermath of the Kishinev pogrom, he worked untiringly to assist its victims, founding the Self-Defense Association, a group that secretly smuggled weapons to endangered Jews in czarist Russia.

But his pacifist inclinations crystallized soon thereafter; in 1917, he opposed American entry into the war, taking a principled stand that was generally at odds with the position of most American Jews. His activity in the American peace movement was an important living testimonial to the vitality of Jewish ideas about peace, although Magnes actually spoke only for a small fraction of the American Jewry at the time. In fact, that was among the reasons that motivated his later decision to settle in Jerusalem, where he became one of the cofounders (1925) of the organization *Brit Shalom* (Covenant of Peace), a pacifist movement that went on to engage in a remarkable attempt to build bridges between Jews and Arabs.

After the bloody riots of August 1929 in Palestine, every bit as violent as earlier pogroms in Russia, Judah Magnes opened the session at Hebrew University with an address that underscored the need for a shared common path to peace among Jews and Arabs:

> One of the greatest cultural obligations of the Jewish
> people is the attempt to come to the Promised Land: not
> by conquest, like Joshua, but traversing the paths of
> peace and culture — by means of arduous physical
> labor and sacrifice, resolute never to take any action
> that cannot be defended before the conscience of the
> world.[8]

Judah Magnes could see only one hope for the country: Jews and Arabs would have to learn to live together — not in land where borders divided one people from another, but in a binational state founded on principles of peace. Magnes was not a philosopher; yet he was a man of *shalom*, able to bring together different factions, an academic who molded the structure of the new university in Jerusalem and succeeded in attracting friends to his political work through the magnetism of his charismatic personality and the ardor of his commitment to his project of peace.

In 1942, he helped found the successor organization to *Brit Shalom*, the *Ihud* (Unity). Its membership included personalities such as Martin Buber, Ernst Simon, Moshe Smilansky, Rabbi Binyamin, and others who had been active in Brit Shalom. Both these organizations were engaged in a constant struggle against the dominant current of the time, and neither apparently enjoyed any great success.

Nonetheless, if we look today at the various initiatives for peace launched within Israel over the past several decades, and their proponents, it may well be that the latter were better able to truly articulate the genuine views of the Israeli population than many of its successive elected governments. This belief in *shalom* was not only the yearning for a life in security and an ultimate end to conflict in the region. Its roots ran deeper and were older, anchored in Judaism and the Jewish state. The thinkers mentioned, many of who had emigrated from Germany, had been significantly influenced by the ideas of Hermann Cohen, Moritz Lazarus (1824—1903) and the entire complex of ideas in Western thought.

---

8. Judah Magnes, Address Opening the Academic Year, 1929/30, Hebrew University, Jerusalem.

We enter an area at this point where recognition has to be given to that vast complex of philosophy, secular messianism, and economic theory lightly labeled "socialism." The interrelationship between Judaism and socialism has been treated extensively on many levels — often in an inimical fashion. One can trace a line of development that moves from Karl Marx to Ernst Bloch, to Ber Borochov and A.D. Gordon (in terms of Zionism), all of it part of an anguished social history not untouched by anti-Semitism. The whole development of the *Bund* (the Jewish Socialist movement in Eastern Europe) should be re-appraised in this last decade of the twentieth century. In our more limited quest for the Jewish concept of peace in our time, we can only acknowledge the influence in Europe and Israel of socialist theory and practice which shaped that quest for peace.[9] Even though the *kibbutz* movement (Jewish collectives in Israel) has moved far away from its founding pioneers with their socialistic ideals (and is indeed rapidly disappearing), much of that utopian vision was part of the quest for peace in Israel, and may yet play a significant role in the coming decades.

So often, the "outsiders" within Jewish and general society were the voices that spoke for peace. In Israel, this thought could be applied to Martin Buber, to Judah Magnes, and to Shmuel Bergmann, even though their teachings of peace became firmly rooted within Jewish thought. But, particularly from the left wing, there were also the non-philosophers, the poets and writers who were or are eloquent prophets of peace. Two examples out of many, again following our theme of the Germanic speaking community, were an Austrian who lived in the Diaspora, and a German living in Israel: the late Erich Fried and the very active Uri Avnery.[10]

Erich Fried was one of the great moral voices of our time. He fled from Vienna, where his father was murdered by the Nazis, and settled in Great Britain, where he worked on

---

9. As William Templer points out, Buber was influenced by Gustav Landauer's utopian anarchism, as were many others in Shomer Ha-Tzair, including its prime theorist A.D. Gordon.

10. Albert H. Friedlander, Riders towards the Dawn: From Pessimism to Tempered Optimism, London, 1993, presents a more extensive treatment of these writers.

behalf of refugees, starved as a factory worker, and soon
established himself as a great poet and translator (he still
starved!). Fried had been an active communist from his
youthful days, and while he eventually broke with the party
he remained very much a Socialist activist, working for
many peace organizations. He later identified himself closely with the Palestinians and their suffering, and became a
harsh critic of Israel. At one time, challenging his own earlier beliefs, he wrote a series of "counter poems," set alongside
his earlier works. Thus, a poem dealing with the Children of
Israel fleeing Egypt was "countered" by a poem describing
the suffering of the Egyptian soldiers in the Sinai desert.

As a committed Communist (which he defined in his own
way), Fried mocked those "intellectuals who imitate the
workers, often intellectuals with a bad conscience who only
recently became Socialists."[11] In that text, fighting particularly against atomic warfare, Fried says that

> Now, we hear "An atomic war would be death." The cue
> word "death" mobilizes our in no way totally self-aware
> patterns of behaviour and causes us to think about
> atomic warfare as little as possible, so that we displace
> such unbearable thoughts . . . but atomic warfare is not
> an avoidable biological catastrophe, but an avoidable
> societal catastrophe . . . workers and intellectuals, even
> those belonging to different classes, can easily come to
> communicate with one another here: desiring to remain
> alive is not a class question.[12]

When Erich Fried considered the more refined methods of
manipulating public thinking, combined with an ever-grow-
ing development of sophisticated atomic weaponry, he saw
this as an even greater danger for peace than the Nazi state.

> Today, in the face of even more refined manipulation-
> techniques and, at the same time, a new development of
> atomic weapons and an unretractable threat of destruc-
> tion — more so than the comparable less dangerously

11. Trans. from Erich Fried, "Anmerkungen zu Verhaltensmustern"
("Notes on Patterns of Behaviour"), in Intellektuelle und
Sozialismus, Berlin, 1968, p. 51.

12. Ibid., p. 36.

armed National-Socialists — it is perhaps even more important, to turn to conscious patterns of behaviour. [13]

Perhaps this was combined with his quite remarkable capacity for reconciliation with the enemies of the past. Fried could sit down with ex-Nazis and with neo-Nazis, quite determined to change their ways of thinking, and without rancor and enmity from his side. Something of a visionary, more of a saint, often dreadfully wrong, he remains one of the great teachers of our time.

There is no standard of judgment by which one can judge Uri Avneri to be gentle, saintly, or even to be a conciliator. At the same time, who but Uri Avneri, publisher of the left-wing *Ha-Olam Ha-zeh*, could actually meet in Beirut with the PLO — Leader Yassir Arafat (in July 1982) and enter into a dialog with him that was later published in a significant book *My Friend, My Enemy*. Avnery, too, is frequently wrong (one thinks of his unjustified attack upon Elie Wiesel after Wiesel's work for peace was honored with the Nobel Peace Prize). He can nonetheless be seen as one of the important voices for peace in the Middle East, as a critic of (any) Israeli government, and as a searcher for truth. In 1991, an important book was published by him in Germany.[14]

The Greek Legend tells the story of the centaur Nessos, who is slain by Hercules with a poisoned arrow. Nessos convinces the wife of Hercules (Deianira) that his blood-drenched garment would renew her husband's love for her if he wears it; but, poisoned, it kills Hercules. Writing after the Gulf War, Avnery sees the occupied territories, Golan Heights, the West Bank, and the Gaza Strip, as a Nessos shirt which Israel must tear off its back if it wants to survive. Israel must come to terms with the Arabs and the Palestinians, both sides must recognize the right to exist for the other, both sides must renounce violence and war; only then will true peace be possible.

In one chapter of his book *Dances with Wolves,* Avnery expresses his belief that the Israeli peace movement died in

---

13. Ibid., p. 87.

14. Trans. from Uri Avneri, Wir tragen das Nessos-Gewand: Israel und der Frieden im Nahen Osten, Bonn, 1991.

the Gulf War. He points to the highly respected leaders of the peace movement — Amos Oz, A.B. Yehoschua, and other distinguished writers who issued a statement in favor of the Gulf War and condemning the German peace movement, which had demonstrated against that war. When the Palestinians supported Saddam Hussein, another Israeli "peacenik," Jossi Sarid, wrote an angry article "From now on, you can look for me!" indicating his break with any dialog. There had been a tiny peace party in Israel, with its members willing to risk prison for talking with Palestinians. The larger group of "doves" had been more careful. That group had consisted of perhaps 10 members of the *Knesset* (the Israeli Parliament), the *Shalom Achshav* ("Peace Now") movement, and various small Peace Institutes. Peace Now, which had been started early in 1978 with an open letter to the public by some officers, and which has drawn support from the USA, is still a force for peace. After the massacre in the camps of Sabra and Shatila, almost 400,000 Israelis demonstrated against the policies of the government and particularly against General Ariel Sharon; but, as Avnery points out, since the beginning of the Intifada (December 1987), the peace movements in Israel have receded. Uri Avnery ponders upon this:

> It is very difficult to "dance with the wolves" in Israel. Every true confrontation with the Palestinians would raise questions which are much too painful: Was Zionism only a Liberation movement? Have our Jewish needs and the Holocaust blinded us to the pain of other people? Are our rights to Eretz Yisrael absolute and exclusive? Are the Palestinians themselves solely responsible for their misfortunes? How did the problem of the Palestinian Refugees really arise? Did Israel truly always desire peace, and was this always, actually, rejected by the Arabs? Fundamentally, doesn't the Intifada have some right on its side?[15]

Perhaps, under the Rabin government, some of these questions are beginning to be explored. In the midst of a volatile political situation, one cannot make clear predictions about the future. It is clear, however, that there are many voices for peace within the land, even if peace move-

---

15. Ibid., p. 84.

ments, at the moment, seem close to impotent. And one must return to the conviction that the Israelis, fashioned within the furnace of affliction, are not as blind to the suffering of the Palestinians as many believe. And a person like Uri Avnery is as representative of the Jewish quest for peace as many Israeli hard-liners.

In the end, we come back to the religious leaders and the philosophers who have sustained the ancient vision of peace within a tradition that might move through various paradigms of thought in each generation, but which builds upon a bedrock of Biblical and rabbinic teachings. Turning once more to Buber, Magnes, and Bergmann, we find that what they have to say is still relevant today. Before we turn to their specific ideas, it is useful to recall that their commitment to peace was not a stance situated on the intellectual periphery in Jewish tradition. In that "old-new" Jewish world of the *yishuv*, there was also a profoundly genuine Orthodox current committed in both belief and in daily practice to the furtherance of *shalom*.

I am thinking here particularly of Rabbi Abraham Isaac Kook (1865—1935), an honored and respected Orthodox rabbinical leader, although regarded by many of his religious contemporaries as an outsider due to his staunch Zionist views. As the Chief Ashkenaz Rabbi in Palestine (1921), it was his conviction that the secular project of (re)settlement in the "Holy Land" was a kind of necessary spadework paving the path for the messianic age — it was, so to speak, the beginning of redemption. His maxim was "what is holy shall be renewed, what is new shall be made holy." The principle of peace lay at the very heart of Rav Kook's teachings. The image of the "priest of war" is found in Deuteronomy 20:2—4:

> Then when fighting impends, the priest must come forward and address the army in these words: "Hear,
> Israel! Now that you are about to join battle with your enemy, do not lose heart or be afraid; do not let alarm affect you, and do not give way to panic in face of them. The Lord your God accompanies you to fight for you against your enemy and give you the victory."[16]

---

16. The Revised English Bible.

This "priest of war," noted Rav Kook, is not endowed with any hereditary office that he can pass on to his son, because no official function in war can be hereditary. The only office that could be handed down from generation to generation is one dedicated to peace, Kook argued, since *shalom* is imbued with such supreme value in Jewish tradition.

It is one of the true ironies of history — and perhaps indicative of the constant battle between the generations — that it was precisely the son of Rav Kook, Zvi Yehuda Kook, who turned most viciously against the teachings of his father. The seminary established by Rav Kook in Jerusalem, the Yeshiva Merkaz Ha-Rav, has become the main center for the development of *Gush Emunim*, which is the wellspring of right-wing religious radicalism, which uses the Biblical texts in order to claim all of the land area in dispute for the Jewish people. What outsiders called the "Occupied Territories" is here called "Judea and Samaria" and seen as the very heart of the Holy Land which Jews have to claim for Israel. The *Gush Emunim* continues to attempt more and more settlements in those areas. Out of Rav Kook's gentle school, a call for *"Eretz Yisrael Shlema"* — *All* of Israel — has emerged in the form of the most militant Orthodox nationalism imaginable. Whether or not one relates this to the militant rejection of *Galut* (exile) thinking, which holds that Israel was forced into a relationship with the surrounding world (which to the militants in Israel is seen as the thinking that led to the destruction of the Jews during the Holocaust); whether or not it is part of a new "fortress mentality" ("Masada will not fall again"; i.e., we will withdraw into our own fortress Israel and will fight off all comers"), the end result is a rejection of any peace initiative, any attempt to trade land for peace, to recognize other claims alongside that of the exclusive claim for the God-given land. Peace does not lie that way.

In the Diaspora (the *galut*, exile), there are gentler voices within Orthodoxy. Dr. Jonathan Sacks, Chief Rabbi of the British Commonwealth, is more representative of an Orthodoxy that feels itself close to total commitment to the Orthodox Israeli stance, but which nevertheless harks back to the position of Rav Kook. In a BBC World Service

Broadcast in October 1992, Dr. Sacks examined a key question in religious law regarding prohibitions on what may be carried on the Sabbath. Is one permitted, for example, to carry a sword? In answering this question, he initially cited rabbinical tradition. The rabbis had concluded that this question could not be answered by a simple "no". During times of peace, when a sword was not needed for defense or attack, it functioned more as an emblem of honor designed to emphasize the dignity of the man who carried it. The rabbis also noted that it might be worn directly attached to one's clothing as an ornament or badge of honor, and that would not be considered an act of "carrying," enjoined on the Sabbath.

Nonetheless, despite its potential ornamentality, the sword, even in times of peace, remains an emblem of war. For that reason, the rabbis ruled that it could not be carried on the Sabbath without desecrating the sacred character of the day.

Viewed from outside, such hair-splitting disputations could be regarded as minor disputes about relatively unimportant matters. In actuality, however, they touch on the very essence of Judaism.

Yet the concept of *shalom* has not exercised such a decisive influence on the thinking of all religiously-minded Jews. One is reminded, for example, of one of the leading rabbis in Israel, who posed for a photograph brandishing a machine-gun in one hand and a Torah scroll in the other. He undoubtedly had the Biblical times of Ezra and Nehemiah in mind, when the builders working on the construction of Jerusalem and the Temple carried both tools and weapons. And the "*shomrim*," the guards in the early kibbutzim, were patterned specifically along this earlier militant Biblical model.

Those are the material conditions of life in Israel, the stark realities of survival. Yet notwithstanding these constant exigencies, it is clear that the concept of peace is still very much alive in Israeli secular and religious life, and that the population yearns for the day when a lasting peace will finally come.

The German thinkers mentioned earlier — Buber, Simon, Leo Baeck — were not always able to exercise a concrete impact on the broader public. Yet their pronouncements on peace constitute a seed that has continued to germinate within Israel and beyond.

Unfortunately, it is impossible in this brief review to do justice to the entire complex of their thinking. But their conceptions of *shalom* indicate just how straight was the path they had chosen to tread. Moreover, they were fully aware of the profound implications of their thought. On October 31, 1921, Martin Buber gave an address on "The Jewish National Home and National Policy in Palestine" that concluded with the following admonition:

> In Palestine, we have not lived together with the Arabs, we have lived alongside them. But a situation where two peoples live side-by-side on the same territory must necessarily degenerate into confrontation if it cannot evolve into a shared togetherness. That eventuality is a threat here too. There is no path leading back to mere side-by-side coexistence. And as formidable as the obstacles may seem, it is still possible to push on to togetherness. I don't know for how long that will still remain an option. But I do know this: if we do not move on to that point, we shall never reach our aspired goal. For the third time now, we are being tested on and by the land"[17]

And in a lecture entitled "Then When?" delivered in Antwerpen in July 1932, Buber said:

> Our sages have taught that the person who creates peace is a partner in God's work. . . . You help to make world peace a reality by acting to realize peace where you feel called upon and summoned to do so: in activity in your own community, where you are able to assist in actively determining the relationship of that community to others. The prophetic message of peace directed to Israel is not only valid for messianic times; it is meant for the day when the people will be called upon anew to participate in the shaping of the fate of its ancient homeland — and is true and valid for today. "If not now, then when?" Fulfillment in the "then" is linked by mysterious strands to fulfillment in the here-and-now.[18]

---

17. Trans. from Martin Buber, Kampf um Israel — Reden und Schriften 1931—32, Berlin, 1933, p. 451.

18. Ibid., pp. 459f.

The concepts of *"shalom"* and the "ancient homeland of Israel" merge together here, a salient fact in considering a state that was conceived in the name of peace, not war. I must reject the notion that the modern State of Israel is basically some sort of heavily armed machine for waging war. On the other hand, one should avoid the other extreme — blindly asserting that Israel is the great paragon of peace in our time. In the wake of the Shoah and its ravages, we are all wounded and maimed, and recovery comes but slowly for the land of Israel and the world.

The English journal *New Outlook* was founded in Israel in 1957; Buber gave it its name and motto: "The time has come for the peoples of the Middle East to acquire a new outlook." Today, this progressive periodical continues to report on the daily work on behalf of peace in Israel. The magazine has dealt with the activities of organizations like *Oz v'Shalom* (Strength and Peace, an Orthodox religious peace movement), the *Neve Shalom* Arab-Jewish village community initiative, and many others. Admittedly, *New Outlook* does not speak for the majority of Israelis. Although Martin Buber is no longer alive, his ideas retain their relevance and topicality. In order to comprehend his thinking about peace, it is necessary to recall that he was not only concerned about relations between the State of Israel and its neighbors. The search for *shalom* in the world, that leitmotif of Jewish life, should not be sought only in the here-and-now, or in a distant messianic era — it also involves the past. When Martin Buber chose to accept the Peace Prize of the German Book Industry and journey to Frankfurt in 1953 to receive it formally, that decision sparked a heated controversy in Israel.

His attitude sheds light on an element of overriding centrality for Jewish thought and life, namely the notion that it is necessary for peace to be manifested in one's innermost attitude vis-à-vis the past as well. In 1989, I wrote:

> Martin Buber's "The Human Path" teaches that every journey to one's fellow man is, first of all, an inward journey into one's own deeper existence. "Rabbi Bunam taught: Our sages have written: 'Seek peace where you dwell.' Peace cannot be sought except in one's own self. The psalmist says: 'There is no peace in my bones

because of my sins. . . .' Only after a person has found
peace within can he go forth to search for peace
throughout the entire world. . . . The recognition of a
turning-point in one's own life and in the life of one's
fellow beings is an inner experience that ultimately
leads us to peace. Individuals live in their own imper-
fection; and sin festers in one's bones until it has been
conquered. This teaching of Buber was passed on to me
through my meeting with the great master; perhaps it
also characterizes my encounter with the Germans
more generally.[19]

Buber's position concerning the concept of peace and its
central importance helped me to grasp the idea that *shalom*
between Germans and Jews can, and indeed, must be confronted and addressed directly — a recognition that was
almost more difficult to accept than Buber's teaching about
the need for peace and reconciliation between Israelis and
Arabs. Yet Helmut Schmidt, in his 1978 speech on "Truthfulness and Tolerance" on the occasion of the fortieth anni-
versary of the November 1938 (Crystal Night) pogroms, was
likewise inspired by a sense of hope he had derived specifically from Buber:

Twenty-five years ago in the Church of St. Paul in
Frankfurt, the German-Jewish philosopher Martin
Buber asked: "Who am I to dare presume I could
forgive here?"[20]

Here, it was not a question of "forgiveness," but only a
simple and unadorned attempt to find peace in the
encounter between persecutors and victims. Although the
victims still suffered from physical and psychological
wounds, there was now a new generation in Germany, free
from any taint of the Nazi past. Admittedly, it remains an
extremely difficult and complicated undertaking to locate a
viable path to peace in the encounter today between
Germans and Jews. Yet this challenge too remains part of
contemporary Jewish existence. Moreover, Buber was not

---

19. Trans from Albert H. Friedlander, Ein Streifen Gold — Auf Wegen
    zur Versöhnung, Munich, 1989, p. 9.

20. Trans. from Albert H. Friedlander, "Begegnung nach vierzig Jahren:
    Deutsche und Juden heute," in Der Monat, Die großen Kontroversen
    II, 1986, p. 17.

the only thinker who travelled that stony path; the name of Leo Baeck (1873—1956) should also be recalled.

A brief comment can suffice, since Leo Baeck's entire life bore concrete testimony to the Jewish conception of *shalom*. It is a little-known fact that Baeck, who can be justifiably regarded as one of the greatest Jewish thinkers of the twentieth century and a major figure in world Reform Judaism, was for a time president of the Jewish Pacifist Society after World War I. Simultaneously, he also held membership in the Association of Jewish War Veterans (Verband jüdischer Soldaten), since he had been a chaplain at the front during World War I.

Baeck stayed on in the Third Reich as president of the beleaguered Reich Association of Jews in Germany, was deported in 1943 to the Theresienstadt concentration camp and managed to survive, relocating to London in 1945; from 1938, Buber had been in Palestine. Nonetheless, both men simultaneously moved toward greater openness in approaching the young German democracy in the early 1950s. A few months before Buber's arrival in 1953 to accept the Peace Prize of the German Book Industry at the Frankfurt Book Fair, Leo Baeck's famous essay "Israel and the German People" appeared in the journal *Merkur* (October 1952). It expressed the hope that peace and reconciliation could be brought one step nearer:

> Only a person motivated by a deep desire — perhaps one might even say an affectionate longing — for inner candor and external clarity should speak about peace between Israel and the German people. Only this truthfulness — where thinking and speech unite into something definite, leaving no place for any afterthoughts or excuses — entitles an individual to affirm or deny, to express hopes or register doubts in this matter.[21]

How can *shalom* be found? It lies in oneself, in one's fellow human beings. Yet only if truthfulness can join together with an honesty in which what is abstract and intellectual is fused with the moral dimension; and where attempts to move toward peace avoid all sentimentality. In Baeck's eyes,

---

21. Ibid., p. 17.

this was the sole practicable path for eventually arriving at a mode of reconciliation between the "Jewish people") and Germany. Just as Buber had asked "If not now, then when?" pertaining to peace between Arabs and Jews in 1932, Leo Baeck confronts us with the analogous question in another situation — the postwar relations between Jews and Germans. Yet here too, peace is also the objective:

> If we assume that this objective and personal founda-
> tion already exists, should the discussion and debate
> about peace be initiated right now? Is the time really
> ripe for this? There's an old Jewish saying: "press the
> hour and it takes flight."[22]

Baeck wrote that in 1952, when virtually no one would have been able to comprehend a so-called "final offer of peace". At a time when the dust and ashes from the concentration camps still lingered in the air, who could even imagine a viable path leading to "peace"? Unless perhaps in that Kantian sense of "eternal peace" — in the graveyard! The shadows of the dead had cast their pall upon the faces of the living. From what vantage was this question posed? Leo Baeck commented:

> These are not questions being asked by an individual
> person. Rather, the act, what was perpetrated and
> inflicted, now poses the question, calling upon the inter-
> rogated to respond. It is not a "he" who asks, but an
> "it." Yet only a "he" can answer here. Human beings,
> individuals, are called upon to confront and deal with
> events, with what has collectively come to pass. What is
> crucial is that the questions be accepted on both sides of
> the divide. Some day, sooner or later, the answer, the
> true answer, will finally be found. That is the hope.[23]

Indeed, his essay concludes on a definite note of hopefulness:

> Two peoples with a shared fate cannot continue indefi-
> nitely to ignore and turn their backs on one other. If
> this peace is examined and prepared for in a spirit of
> honesty — which means not to forget what has tran-
> spired — and is, God willing, finally realized some day,
> it can prove important for all humankind.[24]

---

22. Ibid.
23. Ibid., p. 18.
24. Ibid.

The great probity and moral decency of these two Jewish thinkers join together here in a peace initiative on the plane of thought that is emblematic of our age. The aftermath of the Holocaust is a hard and stony place for such peace to take root — even in a people dedicated to *shalom*, a nation treated so unspeakably by its tormentors that survivors should now be incapable of entertaining any thought of building a new peace. The fact that despite all that has happened, there was nonetheless a Martin Buber in our ranks, a Leo Baeck — this, to my mind, is also a sign, an omen from above. Buber was a committed non-religious Zionist, while Baeck was a committed religious non-Zionist — and both loved the Jewish people. Baeck's final great work, *This People Israel: The Meaning of Jewish Existence*, placed the totality of the Jewish People alongside Judaism. There was no inconsistency in Baeck's life, which included leadership in the Jewish Agency for Palestine and the presidency of the *Keren Ha-Yesod* (building up Jewish settlement in Palestine) as part of his pre-war work in Germany in the 1920s and 1930s.[25]

Since we have included movements and views on peace in Israel within our purview, it is useful to recall the remarks of a colleague of Baeck and Buber on this highly charged context of "Germany-Israel." Commenting on the Germans, Ernst Simon wrote:

> The new Germany can only "come to terms with" its recent past if it is ready to engage in a project geared to a genuine transformation of its ways (*Umkehr*).[26] Such *Umkehr* entails an attempt to reverse and erase, as much as feasible, the consequences of the evil deed. No dead victim will ever be brought back to life, but this process can help contribute to preventing further slaughter and war in the future.

> An energetic peace policy aimed at promoting everything that might bring Israel and its neighbors to reconciliation and understanding would be one possible act in

---

25. See Albert H. Friedlander, *Leo Baeck: Teacher of Theresienstadt*, London, 1973, for a full analysis of Baeck's position.

26. In using the German term "Umkehr," Simon is alluding to the Hebrew concept of "teshuvah" (roughly translatable as "repentance"), a central concept in rabbinical ethics, Jewish philosophy and mysticism over the centuries.

such a process of *Umkehr*. Then the new Israel could, in peace and humanity, continue its project of reconstruction. If they really wish, they should do everything in their power to help all the nations of the world achieve God's peace — including Jews and Arabs in the Holy Land. We Jews have survived as God's witnesses in conditions of supreme suffering and under the most extreme hardship: in our own state, we now hope to be able, as God's witnesses, to live and survive in freedom.[27]

Walter Homolka's study of the idea of peace in Judaism has shed light on the various stages this concept has evolved through over the centuries in Jewish belief and life. It is no surprise that this trajectory of growth traverses the polarities inherent in Jewish thought. Peace is necessarily juxtaposed to war, and Israelis today seem at times to live in a quasi-Biblical situation akin to that of the early Hebrews, and the Jews who suffered under Roman oppression.

Yet Israelis (and Jews everywhere) now share the consciousness of a horrendous experience unknown to Biblical Jewry: the trauma of the Shoah. It is truly a divine dispensation that this concept of *shalom* can continue to survive among the living despite the sheer enormity of this wound. That realization can serve to inspire us with hope for the future, even when we see the shortcomings and militaristic thinking prevalent within Israeli society — indeed, especially when we are cognizant of their powerful presence.

Elie Wiesel, the Nobel Peace laureate, should, I believe, be comprehended within the structures of the Jewish state, even though he takes the whole world as his home, and is engaged in struggles against injustice across the planet. In his Nobel acceptance speech, Wiesel stated:

> Finally, there are also the Palestinians, for whose plight I have sympathy, but whose methods I regret. Violence and terrorism are not the answer. Something must be done for their suffering, and soon. I trust in Israel, because I have faith in the Jewish people. Give Israel a chance, let hatred and danger disappear from its borders, and there shall be peace in and around the Holy

---

27. Trans. from Ernst Akiva Simon, "Das Zeugnis des Judentums," in *Der Monat*, Die großen Kontroversen II, 1986, pp. 23f.

Land. Yes, I have faith. Faith in God and even in His creation. Without that faith it would be impossible to act. And to act is the only remedy against indifference: the most insidious danger of all. Is that not the true meaning of Albert Nobel's legacy? Wasn't his fear of war actually a shield against war? [28]

In Israel and elsewhere, one can see examples of the fear of war functioning as a shield against war. Yet fear can never suffice. Messianic hope and the love of *shalom*, manifest in every Sabbath service, are also integral components of the peace movement within Judaism. As Buber taught: "You create peace by acting to realize peace where you feel called upon and summoned to do so."

An examination of the belief in peace within Jewish tradition must ultimately grapple with the question: is the development of this belief bound up with the essence of Judaism or the existence of the Jewish people? This is an instance of that ancient and central polarity between essence and existence.[29] *Shalom* as concept and dream lives in the Torah, the Bible, in rabbinical interpretations and the laws of the *halacha* as they have evolved over two millennia. Every era struggles against war, and war has been a common occurrence throughout human history. No generation would ever have declared the "god of war" to be the focus of their religion. But every nation engaged in combat, Jewish, Muslim, or Christian, would chose to appropriate the divinity for itself — averring that God was on their side and against the enemy. Chaplains in uniform still patriotically bless the cannons and battleships of their own country. Religion bows down before the might of the state. In the belief system of these religions, the "just war" continues to be a valid and admissible concept, even if the Islamic *jihad*, for example, is conceived of as a just war against unbelief and evil.

Unfortunately, it is the Other who is always regarded as "evil," and the belief in war, seemingly ineradicable, lives on in the world's religions side by side with the concept of peace. Perhaps for that reason, true *shalom* remains a com-

---

28. Trans from Elie Wiesel, Den Frieden feiern, Freiburg, 1991, p. 110.

29. Homolka 1992

ponent of the messianic age, appearing to the observer as
somewhat remote, the ultimate though distant goal.

Nonetheless, the idea of peace plays a special and vital
role within traditional Judaism. Every Sabbath, observant
Jews wish their compatriots a "peaceful Sabbath": "*Shabbat
shalom!*" Prayers in the synagogues constantly speak of the
peace to be found there — a peace bound to realization in
the world. Every Friday evening, the Sabbath is ushered in
by greeting the "angels of peace" — "*malachei ha-shalom*" —
and Jews live in the hope that man, in cooperation with
God, will create peace on earth.

But there is also a strong consciousness that only within
a just society can peace be achieved. Perhaps that is one reason why, in Israel and around in the world, there are so
many Jews active in groups committed to the struggle for
peace and justice. Here we can discern a further development of ideas contained in the Bible: the belief that in the
end of days, all human beings will come to the holy mountain where the lion and lamb shall lie down together, as
envisioned in Micah 4 and Isaiah 11.

Jews, Christians, and Moslems find peace where they
engage in the active struggle against the scourge of war and
the fight for greater justice. For that reason too, it is fitting
to conclude this book with a quote from Elie Wiesel, who
journeyed to the war-ravaged Balkans to see first-hand the
battlefield that was once Yugoslavia:

> It is certain that conditions everywhere are terrible. . . .
> Journalists and representatives of civil rights organiza-
> tions have reported about horrible atrocities. On the one
> hand, Moslems are being massacred by Serbs; on the
> other, Serbs are the victims of Moslem revenge. And
> everywhere it is the civilians who suffer the most: their
> houses are being leveled, their homes burned to the
> ground, entire families suffering from hunger and thirst.
> Everywhere you can hear the cries of wounded orphans,
> see the tears of widows. How, faced with so much human
> suffering, can anyone remain unmoved? . . . Let us not
> forget: each passing day means further deaths.[30]

30. Trans. from Elie Wiesel, "Gleichgültigkeit führt zu Schuld," in Die
Welt, 27th October, 1992, p. 7.

There are echoes here of Amos and Hosea, and of Biblical prophecy more generally — a discourse that must be heard and listened to before *shalom* can ever gain any genuine and enduring hold in our beleaguered world.

We have not yet travelled all the way through the gate of perfection; but it has been a long journey within the Jewish tradition, and we have followed the golden thread of peace described by the ancient rabbis: *"Ohev Shalom, v'rodef shalom"* — love peace and pursue it. The Esaiah and Jeremiah tried in vain to convince the leaders of Israel that peace was the only way of survival for a country surrounded by armed enemies. Today, again within a situation of empowerment, Israel seems caught in the same trap: her enemies can lose many wars, Israel cannot afford to lose one war. At the same time, peace is the only way for the survival of a people and a land where the great teachings of peace emerged. And it is clear that the yearning for peace is part of all Jewish life, throughout the world. In every synagogue in the world, throughout the year, there comes the moment when the descendants of the priests or the rabbi stand in front of the congregation and pronounce the priestly benediction (Numbers 6:24—26):

> May the lord bless you and keep you; may the lord
> make his face shine upon you and be gracious unto you;
> may the lord lift up his countenance upon you, and give
> you *shalom* — peace!

There came a time, in September of 1993, when it seemed to the world that this ancient Priestly Benediction had come closer to realization. Against all odds, in the face of intense pressure on both the Arab and the Israeli leaders to reject any compromise, a meeting took place in Washington, at the White House. To the astonishment of the world, Yasir Arafat and Yitzchak Rabin signed an accord that committed both sides to explore avenues toward peace. They even shook hands — although it seemed to the millions watching that President Clinton had to push Rabin closer to Arafat, and both men's body language proclaimed a continuing distrust and reluctance. But the paper was signed.

It is quite possible that these accords will quickly be overtaken by other events, new explosions of enmity, and that

peace will be farther away from the troubled land in 1994
then it is at this point. Nevertheless, the full texts should be
preserved, even though one must read them more as political
statements than as expressions of a philosophy or a theology. It is at least an indication that the search and yearning
for peace exists on both sides of this anguished confrontation. But one still asks, as the days pass and no significant,
major improvements take place: What prompted these two
leaders to sign the agreement? Was it once again a "Begin-
Sadat moment"? Will it be a turning point in the relationship between Arabs and Jews?

Why did they sign? It seems clear that Arafat, indeed, had
little choice. His mistake in supporting Saddam Hussein
had bankrupted the PLO. He and his organization could do
little to support the suffering Palestinians since the money
sources from the Arab world upon which he depended had
dried up almost completely. As an instinctive survivor, he
knew that he had to take a radical step along the lines of
Sadat, even though he must have been fully aware that this
would also expose him to the fate of that martyr of peace.
Where he had been seen as the "veritable devil" by the
Israelis, he would now have that image in most of the Arab
world. Still, this step toward peace was the most constructive and hopeful action possible for him.

The reasons for Rabin's signing were more complex. As an
intelligent politician, with a view of world affairs, he knew
that the only battles the Palestinians had won — and they
were important ones — were in the field of propaganda.
Much of the world now viewed Israel as the aggressor, as
the oppressor living in a land that somehow was the homeland of the Palestinians. The world Jewish community had
not wavered in their support of Israel, and had understood
the dangers facing Israel from inside and outside. But world
Jewry has less of a sense of isolation, perhaps less of a perspective regarding the dangers confronting Israeli citizens
every day. Moreover, the Jews of the Diaspora take on the
patterns of thinking and general responses of the lands in
which they live. This is particularly true in the Western
lands, where Jews have become acculturated to the democratic societies where they were born and where they feel

totally at home. Anti-Semites sometimes complain of the undue influence Jews have in the United States; but the fact is that it is America itself that influences and shapes the thinking of its Jewish citizens — and American public thinking wants peace and expects the "people of the Book" to be leaders in the quest for peace. Rabin's proposals — Jericho and the Gaza strip — was calculated to make an impact upon the world and also upon the Palestinians.

It is not as though the Palestinians see these as major concessions. The Gaza strip has always been a problematic acquisition, with its economic and social needs that Israel could not supply fully, but which nevertheless drained away needed resources from Israel. It was an open wound, and to the Israelis at least seemed to be incurable. For the Palestinians it also presented problems, since it is isolated from the West Bank; but it was at least an offer, an opening where only a bleak wall had existed. It could be seen as the beginning of negotiations. Jericho seemed a strange offer, compared with a much more politically active town like Nablus, for example, but in retrospect one can see it as an intelligent, fascinating gamble on the road toward peace. Nablus is the first town reached after crossing the Allenby bridge. Anyone traveling toward this area of Palestinian life may well be filled with new hope upon entering the historic town, which could foreshadow peaceful co-existence between Israelis and Palestinians. The "fall of the wall of Jericho" thus becomes a positive statement. The people who live in these areas of concession may well have more positive attitudes toward this leap toward an agreement than the pundits who see all of the problems. Six month after the declaration, pessimists like Edward Said (who condemned the agreement) may well be proven right — but for the wrong reasons. The yearning for peace that lives within the Israeli and the Palestinian people may have been frustrated by the political and even philosophical thinking of those who see themselves as "the leaders." Wrong decisions can always be made. It is still a reality of the deep yearning for peace that characterizes the people of Israel and the displaced Palestinians that found expression on that September morning in Washington, in front of the White House.

Let us say then — even if this moment of possible peace were to be destroyed by the events that follow it, or by the lethargy that afflicts the good, and the fanaticism that afflicts the destroyers of this world — that the accord signed on the 13th of September 1993 should be part of any recorded attempt to chart the course of peace within our society. *JADE (Jewish Arab Dialogue in Europe)* is a publication that appears in London and represents a concerned effort to develop such a dialog. In October 1993 it published the complete PLO-Israel Accord as drawn from various sources. Seen in the light of subsequent events, the text signed in Washington may appear curiously optimistic. The wording concerning elections, transfer of powers, and future negotiations was, of necessity, kept vague and imprecise. Israeli fears and Arab demands clash underneath almost every line of the text, and many of the most important areas — notably Jerusalem — are covered by silence and remain unresolved.

In November 1993 I talked with an Israeli diplomat: the Ambassador at the Court of St. James in London, Moshe Raviv. The ambassador had been involved in much of the earlier negotiations before he came to London in October. What impressed me most was his firm conviction that the signed agreement constituted an irrevocable step forward, and that it was expressive of the deep desire for peace among the Jews and the Palestinians. Ambassador Ravit felt that the processes that had been initiated in that moment of history would move forward quite slowly, and that there would be disappointments. But he also saw that the events that took place were not simply the result of political realities; they expressed the vision of peace that had been part of the life of the people Israel for almost 4,000 years. And we should read the peace accord with this in mind.

Much of the agreement appears cumbersome and dry; but it is, in effect, dynamite. The reactions within Jewish life have divided much of Jewish communal life. The Hassidic Lubavitch community has fought bitterly against this agreement, spending millions in its efforts to undermine, deny, and cancel it. The fight is based upon "religious" suppositions: *all* of the land has been promised by God, and it is a *hillul ha-shem,* a desecration of God's name, to surrender one inch of the Promised Land. The fact that the people of the Land yearn for peace, and that the majority accept the notion that one can trade land for life, land for peace, is totally unacceptable to that religious community, which looks toward the messianic time ahead and ignores the reality of the world where children of Abraham — Palestinians *and* Israelis — must live together and are both loved by God.

In a strange way, the more secular Jew and Arab seem closer to the religious vision of peace. In a recent television program "My Homeland, Your Homeland" (broadcast on BBC in London October 26, 1993), an Israeli and an Arab reacted directly to the Washington agreement and walked through this land with the text of the agreement as their itinerary. Amos Oz, the novelist, and the Palestinian academic Hisham Sharabi visited the Gaza Strip, the Temple mount, the Golan Heights, and the West Bank. Sharabi had not visited his birthplace since 1947, and Amos Oz could introduce him to a Jewish world that had been completely closed to the PLO ideology. And the Palestinian, in turn, gave the Israeli novelist an opportunity to meet Palestinian militants with whom he finally talk. How much the PLO thinker could really gain from a confrontation with the Orthodox Jews remains an open question, and the same could be said about Oz and his encounters. But, after the Washington agreement, the two could at least explore dialog and hope for some resolution, no matter how far apart they were. They, rather than the fanatical defenders of the faith on both sides, decide on the future of peace in Israel. Amos Oz is a voice for peace that rises out of the authentic Jewish tradition of peace which has endured through the millennia, and which received support when Arafat and Rabin shook hands.

This, then, is the end of our short exploration of the vision of peace that has been part of Jewish life, accompanying a people through the dark valleys of our civilizations, pausing occasionally on mountaintops and then plunging once more into the darkest valleys. The peace accord between Israelis and Palestinians left us in a political area that is far more frail, despite the prejudices of our society, than the theologies and philosophies of those who are trapped within the field of politics.

All we can do in a discussion about peace is to affirm hope: hope in God, hope in a world given to humans who must become aware of their task to fashion a better world. And so we return to the prophets, to Amos and Hosea, to Jeremiah and Isaiah. Their central vision has burned itself into the Jewish soul: There cannot be peace without justice; and the sword comes into the world when justice is perverted and is delayed. Peace then becomes the work of human hands; at that point, it becomes a blessing from God.

Appendix

The PLO-Israel Accord, 13 September 1993

Here is the text of the accord signed on Monday 13 September 1993 by the PLO and Israeli representatives. According to the Los Angeles Times of 14 September (from which this is transcribed), it is a translation from a Hebrew text that was itself a translation from the English original. The official text has not been released as of 14 September, but Israeli officials have confirmed the accuracy of this version. This transcription is by Don Bashford but is based on a transcript of an earlier copy by Fayez Abu-Hilal. Don Bashford has checked the Abu-Hilal transcript against the LA Times version.

DECLARATION OF PRINCIPLES ON INTERIM SELF-GOVERNMENT ARRANGEMENTS

The Government of the State of Israel and the PLO (in the Jordanian-Palestinian delegation to the Middle East Peace Conference) (the Palestinian delegation), representing the Palestinian people agree that it is time to put an end to decades of confrontation and conflict, recognize their mutual legitimate and political rights, and strive to live in peaceful coexistence and mutual dignity and security to achieve a just, lasting and comprehensive peace settlement and historic reconciliation through the agreed political process. Accordingly, the two sides agree to the following principles.

ARTICLE I: Aim of the Negotiations

The aim of the Israeli-Palestinian negotiations within the current Middle East peace process is, among other things, to establish a Palestinian Interim Self-Government Authority, the elected Council (the "Council" for the Palestinian people in the West Bank and the Gaza Strip), for a transitional period not exceeding five years, leading to a permanent settlement based on Security Council Resolutions 242 and 338. It is understood that the interim arrangements are an integral part of the whole peace process and that the negotiations on the permanent status will lead to the implementation of Security Council Resolution 242 and 338.

ARTICLE II: Framework for the Interim Period

The agreed framework for the interim period is set forth in this declaration of principles.

ARTICLE III: Elections

1. In order that the Palestinian people in the West Bank and Gaza Strip may govern themselves according to democratic principles, direct, free and general political elections will be held for the Council under agreed supervision and international observation, while Palestinian police will ensure public order.

2. An agreement will be concluded on the exact mode and conditions of the elections in accordance with the protocol attached as Annex I , with the goal of holding the elections not later than nine months after the entry into force of this Declaration of Principles.

3. These elections will constitute a significant interim preparatory step toward the realization of the legitimate rights of the Palestinian people and their just requirements.

ARTICLE IV: Jurisdiction

Jurisdiction of the Council will cover West Bank and Gaza Strip territory, except for issues that will be negotiated in the permanent status negotiations. The two sides view the West Bank and Gaza Strip as a single territorial unit, whose integrity will be preserved during the interim period.

ARTICLE V: Transitional Period and Permanent Status Negotiations

1. The five-year transitional period will begin upon the withdrawal from the Gaza Strip and Jericho area.

2. Permanent status negotiations will commence as soon as possible, but not later than the beginning of the third year of the interim period between the Government of Israel 'and the Palestinian people representatives.

3. It is understood that these negotiations shall cover remaining issues, including: Jerusalem, refugees, settlements, security arrangements, borders, relations and cooperation with other neighbors, and other issues of common interest.

4. The two parties agree that the outcome of the permanent status negotiations should not be prejudiced or pre-empted by agreements reached for the interim period.

ARTICLE VI: Preparatory Transfer of Power and Responsibilities

1. Upon the entry into force of this Declaration of Principles and withdrawal from the Gaza Strip and the Jericho area, a transfer of authority from Israeli military government and its Civil Administration to the authorized Palestinians for this task, as detailed herein, will commence. This transfer of authority will be of preparatory nature until the inauguration of the Council.

2. Immediately after the entry into force of this Declaration of Principles and the withdrawal from the Gaza Strip and the Jericho area, with the view of promoting economic development in the West Bank and Gaza Strip, authority will be transferred to the Palestinians on the following spheres: education and culture, health, social welfare, direct taxation, and tourism. The Palestinian side will commence in building the Palestinian police force, as agreed upon. Pending the inauguration of the Council, the two parties may negotiate the transfer of additional powers and responsibilities, as agreed upon.

ARTICLE VII: Interim Agreement

1. The Israeli and Palestinian delegations will negotiate an agreement on the interim period (the "Interim Agreement").

2. The Interim Agreement shall specify, among other things, the structure of the Council, the number of its members, and the transfer of powers and responsibilities from the Israeli military government and its Civil Administration on the Council. The Interim Agreement shall also specify the Council's executive authority, legislative authority in accordance with Article IX below, and the independent Palestinian judicial organs.

3. The Interim Agreement shall include arrangements, to be implemented upon the inauguration of the Council, for the assumption by the Council of all of the powers and responsibilities transferred previously in accordance with Article VI above.

4. In order to enable the Council to promote economic growth, upon its inauguration, the Council will establish, among other things, a Palestinian Electricity Authority, a Gaza Sea Port Authority, a Palestinian Development Bank, a Palestinian Export Promotion Board, a Palestinian Environmental Authority, a Palestinian Land Authority and a Palestinian Water Administration Authority, and many other authorities agreed upon, in accordance with the Interim Agreement that will specify their powers and responsibilities.

5. After the inauguration of the Council, the Civil Administration will be dissolved, and the Israeli military government will be withdrawn.

ARTICLE VIII: Public Order and Security

In order to guarantee public order and internal security for the Palestinians of the West Bank and Gaza Strip, the Council will establish a strong police force, while Israel will continue to carry the responsibility for defending against external threats, as well as the responsibility for overall security of Israelis for the purpose of safeguarding their internal security and public order.

ARTICLE IX: Laws and Military Orders

1. The Council will be empowered to legislate, in accordance with the Interim Agreement, within all authorities transferred to it.

2. Both parties will review jointly laws and military orders presently in force in remaining spheres.

ARTICLE X: Joint Israel-Palestinian Liaison Committee

In order to provide for a smooth implementation of this Declaration of Principles and any subsequent agreements pertaining to the interim period, upon the entry into force of this Declaration of Principles, a Joint Israel-Palestinian Liaison Committee will be established in order to deal with issues requiring coordination, other issues of common interest, and disputes.

ARTICLE XI: Israeli-Palestinian Cooperation in Economic Fields

Recognizing the mutual benefit of cooperation in promoting the development of the West Bank, the Gaza Strip and Israel, upon the entry into force of this Declaration of Principles, an Israeli-Palestinian Economic Cooperation Committee will be established in order to develop and implement in a cooperative manner the programs identified in the protocols attached as Annex III and Annex IV.

ARTICLE XII: Liaison and Cooperation with Jordan and Egypt

The two parties will invite the Governments of Jordan and Egypt to participate in establishing further liaison and cooperation arrangements between the Government of Israel and the Palestinian representatives on one hand, and the Governments of

Jordan and Egypt, on the other hand, to promote cooperation between them. These arrangements will include the constitution of a Continuing Committee that will decide by agreement on the modalities of admission of persons displaced from the West Bank and Gaza Strip in 1967, together with necessary measures to prevent disruption and disorder. Other matters of common concern will be dealt with by the Committee.

ARTICLE XIII: Redeployment of Israeli Forces

1. After the entry into force of this Declaration of Principles, and not later than the eve of elections for the Council, a redeployment of Israeli military forces in the West Bank and the Gaza Strip will taken place, in addition to withdrawal of Israeli forces carried out in accordance with Article XIV.

2. In redeploying its military forces, Israel will be guided by the principle that its military forces should be redeployed outside populated areas.

3. Further redeployments to specified locations will be gradually implemented commensurate with the assumption of responsibility for public order and internal security by the Palestinian police force pursuant to Article VIII above.

ARTICLE XIV: Israeli Withdrawal from the Gaza Strip and Jericho Area

Israel will withdraw from the Gaza Strip and Jericho area, as detailed in the protocol attached as Annex II.

ARTICLE XV: Resolution of Disputes

1. Disputes arising out of the application or interpretation of the Declaration of Principles, or any subsequent agreements pertaining on the interim period, shall be resolved by negotiations through the Joint Liaison Committee to be established pursuant to Article X above.

2. Disputes which cannot be settled by negotiations may be resolved by a mechanism of conciliation to be agreed upon by the parties.

3. The parties may agree to submit to arbitration [of] disputes relating to the interim period, which cannot be settled through reconciliation. To this end, upon the agreement of both parties will establish an Arbitration Committee.

ARTICLE XVI: Israeli-Palestinian Cooperation Concerning Regional Programs

Both parties view the multilateral working groups as an appropriate instrument for promoting a "Marshall Plan," the regional programs and other programs, including special programs for the West Bank and Gaza Strip, as indicated in the protocol attached as Annex IV.

ARTICLE XVII: Miscellaneous Provisions

1. This Declaration of Principles will enter into force one month after its signing.

2. All protocols annexed to this Declaration of Principles and Agreed Minutes pertaining thereto shall be regarded as an integral part hereof.

ANNEX I: Protocol on the Mode and Conditions of Elections

1. Palestinians of Jerusalem who live there will have the right to participate in the election process, according to an agreement between the two sides.

2. In addition, the election agreement should cover, among other things, the following issues:

(a) the system of election

(b) the mode of the agreed supervision and international observation and their personal composition; and

(c) rules and regulations regarding election campaign, including agreed arrangements for the organizing of mass media, and the possibility of licensing a broadcasting and TV station.

3. The future status of displaced Palestinians who were registered on 4th June 1967 will not be prejudiced because they are unable to participate in the elections process due to practical reasons.

ANNEX II: Protocol on Withdrawal of Israeli Forces from the Gaza Strip and Jericho Area

1. The two sides will conclude and sign within two months from the date of entry into force of this Declaration of Principles, an agreement on the withdrawal of Israeli military forces from the Gaza Strip and the Jericho area. This agreement will include comprehensive arrangements to apply in the Gaza Strip and the Jericho area subsequent to the Israeli withdrawal.

2. Israel will implement an accelerated and scheduled withdrawal of Israeli military forces from the Gaza Strip and Jericho area, beginning immediately with the signing of the agreement on the Gaza Strip and Jericho area and to be completed within a period not exceeding four months after the signing of this agreement.

3. The above agreement will include, among other things:

(a) Arrangements for a smooth and peaceful transfer of authority from the Israeli military government and its Civil Administration to the Palestinian representatives.

(b) Structure, powers and responsibilities of the Palestinian authority in these areas, except: external security, settlements, Israelis, foreign relations, and other mutually agreed matters.

(c) Arrangements for the assumption of internal security and public order by the Palestinian police force consisting of police officers recruited locally and from abroad (holding Jordanian passports and Palestinian documents issued by Egypt). Those who will participate in the Palestinian police force coming from abroad should be trained as police and police officers.

(d) A temporary international or foreign presence, as agreed upon.

(e) Establishment of a joint Palestinian-Israeli Coordination and Cooperation Committee for mutual security purposes.

(f) An economic development and stabilization program, including the establishment of an Emergency Fund, to encourage foreign investment, and financial and economic support. Both sides will coordinate and cooperate jointly and unilaterally with regional and international parties to support these aims.

(g) Arrangements for a safe passage for persons and transportation between the Gaza Strip and Jericho area.

4. The above agreement will include arrangements for coordination between both parties regarding passages:

(a) Gaza-Egypt; and

(b) Jericho-Jordan

5. The offices responsible for carrying out the powers and responsibilities of the Palestinian authority under this Annex II and Articles VI of the Declaration of Principles will be located in the Gaza Strip and in the Jericho area pending the inauguration of the Council.

6. Other than these agreed arrangements, the status of the Gaza Strip and Jericho area will continue to be an integral part of the West Bank and Gaza Strip, and will not be changed in the interim period.

ANNEX III: Protocol on Israeli-Palestinian Cooperation in Economic and Development Programs

The two sides agree to establish an Israeli-Palestinian Continuing Committee for Economic Cooperation, focusing, among other things, on the following:

1. Cooperation in the field of water, including a Water Development Program prepared by experts from both sides, which will also specify the mode of cooperation in the management of water resources in the West Bank and Gaza Strip, and will include proposals for studies and plans on water rights of each party, as well as on the equitable utilization of joint water resources for implementation in and beyond the interim period.

2. Cooperation in the field of electricity, including an Electricity Development Program, which will also specify the mode of cooperation for the production, maintenance, purchase and sale of electricity resources.

3. Cooperation in the field of energy, including an Energy Development Program, which will provide for the exploitation of oil and gas for industrial purposes, particularly in the Gaza Strip and the Negev, and will encourage further joint exploitation of other energy resources. This program may also provide for the construction of a petrochemical industrial complex in the Gaza Strip and the construction of oil and gas pipelines.

4. Cooperation in the field of finance, including a Financial Development and Action Program for the encouragement of international investment in the West Bank and the Gaza Strip, and in Israel, as well as the establishment of a Palestinian Development Bank.

5. Cooperation in the field of transport and communications, including a program, which will define guidelines for the establishment of a Gaza Sea Port area, and will provide for the establishing of transport and communications lines to and from the West Bank and the Gaza Strip to Israel and to other countries. In addition, this program will provide for carrying out the necessary construction of roads, railways, communications lines, etc.

6. Cooperation in the field of trade, including studies, and Trade Promotion Programs, which will encourage local, regional and interregional trade, as well as a feasibility study of crating free trade zones in the Gaza Strip and in Israel, mutual access to these zones, and cooperation in other areas related to trade and commerce.

7. Cooperation in the field of industry, including Industrial Development Programs, which will provide for the establishment of

joint Israeli-Palestinian Industrial Research and Development Centers, will promote Palestinian-Israeli joint ventures, and provide guidelines for cooperation in the textile, food, pharmaceutical, electronics, diamonds, computer and science-based industries.

8. A program for cooperation in, and regulation of, labor relations and cooperation in special welfare issues.

9. A Human Resources Development and Cooperation Plan, providing for joint Israeli-Palestinian workshops and seminars, and for the establishment of joint vocational training centers, research institutes and data banks.

10. An environmental Protection Plan, providing for joint and/or coordinated measure in this sphere.

11. A program for developing coordination and cooperation in the field of communication and media.

12. Any other programs of mutual interest.

ANNEX IV: Protocol on Israeli-Palestinian Cooperation Concerning Regional Development Programs

1. The two sides will cooperate in the context of the multilateral peace efforts in promoting a development program for the region, including the West Bank and the Gaza Strip, to be initiated by the G-7. The parties will request the G-7 to seek the participation in this program of other interested states, such as members of the Organization for Economic Cooperation and Development, regional Arab states and institutions, as well as members of the private sector.

2. The Development Program will consist of two elements:

(a) an Economic Development Program for the West Bank and Gaza Strip.

(b) a Regional Economic Development Program.

(A) The Economic Development Program for the West Bank and the Gaza Strip will consist of the following elements:

1. A Social Rehabilitation Program, including a Housing and Construction Program.

2. A Small and Medium Business Development Plan.

3. An Infrastructure Development Program (water, electricity, transportation and communications, etc.)

4. A Human Resources Plan.

5. Other programs.

(B) The Regional Economic Development Program may consist of the following elements:

1. The establishment of a Middle East Development Fund, as a first step, and a Middle East Development Bank, as a second step.

2. The development of a joint Israeli-Palestinian-Jordanian Plan for coordinated exploitation of the Dead Sea area.

3. The Mediterranean Sea (Gaza) - Dead Sea Canal.

4. Regional Desalination and other water development projects.

5. A regional plan for agricultural development, including a coordinated regional effort for the prevention of desertification.

6. Interconnection of electricity grids.

7. Regional cooperation for the transfer, distribution and industrial exploitation of gas, oil and other energy resources.

8. A Regional Tourism, Transportation and Telecommunications Development Plan.

9. Regional cooperation in other spheres.

3. The two sides will encourage the multi-lateral working groups, and will coordinate towards its success. The two parties will encourage inter-sessional activities, as well as prefeasibility and feasibility studies, within the various multilateral working groups.

AGREED MINUTES TO THE DECLARATION
OF PRINCIPLES ON
INTERIM SELF-GOVERNMENT ARRANGEMENTS

A. General Understandings and Agreements

Any powers and responsibilities transferred to the Palestinians pursuant to the Declaration of Principles prior to the inauguration of the Council will be subject to the same principles pertaining to Article IV, as set out in these Agreed Minutes below.

B. Specific Understandings and Agreements

Article IV. It is understood that:

1. Jurisdiction of the Council will cover West Bank and Gaza Strip territory, except for issues that will be negotiated in the permanent

status negotiations: Jerusalem, settlements, military locations, and Israelis.

2. The Council's jurisdiction will apply with regard to the agreed powers, responsibilities, spheres and authorities transferred to it.

Article VI(2). It is agreed that the transfer of authority will be as follows:

1. The Palestinian side will inform the Israeli side of the names of the authorized Palestinians who will assume the powers, authorities and responsibilities that will be transferred to the Palestinians according to the Declaration of Principles in the following fields: education and culture, health, social welfare, direct taxation, tourism and any other authorities agreed upon.

2. It is understood that the rights and obligations of these offices will not be affected.

3. Each of the spheres described above will continue to enjoy existing budgetary allocations in accordance with arrangements to be mutually agreed upon. These arrangements also will provide for the necessary adjustments required in the order to take into account the taxes collected by the direct taxation office.

4. Upon the execution of the Declaration of Principles, the Israeli and Palestinian delegations will immediately commence negotiations on a detailed plan for the transfer of authority on the above offices in accordance with the above understandings and responsibilities not transferred to the Council.

Article VII(2). The Interim Agreement will also include arrangements for coordination and cooperation.

Article VII(5). The withdrawal of the military government will not prevent Israel from exercising the powers a

Article VIII. It is understood that the Interim Agreement will include arrangements for cooperation and coordination between the two parties in this regard. It is also agreed that the transfer of powers and responsibilities to the Palestinian police will be accomplished in a phased manner, as agreed in the Interim Agreement.

Article X. It is agreed that, upon the entry into force of the Declaration of Principles, the Israeli and Palestinian delegations will exchange the names of the individuals designated by them as members of the Joint Israeli-Palestinian Liaison Committee. It is further agreed that each side will have an equal number of members in the Joint Committee. The Joint Committee will reach decisions by agreement. The Joint Committee may add other technicians and experts, as necessary. The Joint Committee will decide on the frequency and place or places of its meetings.

Annex I. It is understood that, subsequent to the Israeli withdrawal, Israel will continue to be responsible for external security, and for internal security and public order of settlements and Israelis. Israeli military forces and civilians may continue to use roads freely within the Gaza Strip and the Jericho area.

Bibliography

Allerhand, Jacob, *Das Judentum in der Aufklärung,* Stuttgart/Bad Cannstatt, 1980.

Assembly of Rabbis of the Reform Synagogues of Great Britain, *Forms of Prayer for Jewish Worship I,* London, 1977 (7th Edition).

Avneri, Uri, *Wir tragen das Nessos-Gewand: Israel und der Frieden im Nahen Osten,* Bonn, 1991.

Baeck, Leo, *Das Wesen des Judentums,* Wiesbaden, n.d.

—, *Aus drei Jahrtausenden: Wissenschaftliche Untersuchungen und Abhandlungen zur Geschichte des jüdischen Glaubens,* Tübingen, 1958.

Bamberger, Selig (Ed.), *Raschi-Kommentar zum Pentateuch,* Basel, 1975.

Bammel, Fritz, *Die Religionen der Welt und der Friede auf Erden — eine religionsphänomenologische Studie,* Munich, 1957.

Benamozegh, Elia, *Le crime de la guerre denoncé à l'humanité,* Livorno, n.d.

Bertholet, Alfred, *Wörterbuch der Religionen,* Stuttgart, 1976.

Boehlich, Walter (ed.), *Der Berliner Antisemitismusstreit* (Quellensammlung), Frankfurt am Main, 1965.

Borowitz, Eugene B., *Reform Judaism Today,* Vols. 1—4, New York, 1978.

Brandt, Henry G. (ed.), *Or Chadash — Gebete für Schabbat, Fest- und Wochentage,* Zurich, 1981.

Buber, Martin, *Kampf um Israel — Reden und Schriften 1931—33,* Berlin, 1933.

—, *Des Baal-Schem-Tow Unterweisung im Umgang mit Gott,* Cologne, 1970.

Caspari, Wilhelm, *Der biblische Friedensgedanke nach dem Alten Testament,* Berlin-Lichterfelde, 1916.

Charles, R.H. (ed.), *The Apokrypha and Pseudepigrapha of the Old Testament in English,* Oxford, 1913.

Charles, R.H. (trans.), *The Book of Enoch,* London, 1980 (7th Impression).

Cohen, Arthur A. (ed.), *Essays from Martin Buber's Journal "Der Jude" 1916—1928*, Alabama, 1980.

Cohen, Hermann, *Liebe und Gerechtigkeit in den Begriffen Gott und Mensch — Jahrbuch für jüdische Geschichte und Literatur*, Vol. 3, Berlin, 1900.

—, *Innere Beziehungen der Kantischen Philosophie zum Judentum*, 28th Annual Report of the *Lehranstalt für die Wissenschaft des Judentums*, Berlin,1910.

—, *Jüdische Schriften*, Vol. 3, Berlin, 1924.

—, *Religion der Vernunft aus den Quellen des Judentums*, Wiesbaden, 1978.

Cohon, Samuel S., *Judaism and War — Popular Studies in Judaism*, Cincinnati, Ohio, n.d.

Cronbach, Abraham, "World Peace and the Individual Jew," in Bulletin No. 18, World Union for Progressive Judaism, London, January 1948.

Davidson, Benjamin, *The Analytical and Chaldee Lexicon*, London, 1970.

Davidson, Israel (ed.), *Selected Religious Poems of Solomon ibn Gabirol*, Philadelphia, 1974.

Dresner, Samuel H., *God, Man and Atomic War*, New York, 1966.

Dubnow, Simon, *Weltgeschichte des Jüdischen Volkes*, 3 Vols., Jerusalem, 1971 (2nd edition).

Eban, Abba, *Dies ist mein Volk — Die Geschichte der Juden*, Munich/Zurich, 1970.

Eichhorn, David Max, *Conversion to Judaism — A History and Analysis*, New York, 1965.

Eisler, Moritz, *Vorlesungen über die jüdischen Philosophen des Mittelalters*, Vols, 1—3, Vienna, 1870—1883 (Reprint).

Elbogen, Ismar, *Der Edle sinnt auf Edles — Preisarbeit No. IV der Moritz-Mannheimer-Stiftung der Großloge für Deutschland aus dem Compendium "Friedenspflichten des Einzelnen,"* Gotha, 1917.

—, *Der jüdische Gottesdienst in seiner geschichtlichen Entwicklung*, (7th edition) Hildesheim, 1967.

Encyclopaedia Judaica, Vol. 13, Cols. 194—199, Jerusalem, 1971.

Fohrer, Georg, *Das Alte Testament*, Teil 1, Gütersloh, 1980 (3rd Edition).

Frankel, Zacharias, *Der gerichtliche Beweis nach mosaisch-talmudischem Rechte*, Berlin, 1846.

Fried, Erich, *Intellektuelle und Sozialismus*, Berlin, 1968.

Friedlander, Albert Hoschander, *Riders towards the Dawn: From Pessimism to Tempered Optimism*, London 1993.

——, "Begegnung nach vierzig Jahren: Deutsche und Juden heute," in *Der Monat, Die großen Kontroversen II*, 1986.

——, *Ein Streifen Gold — Auf Wegen zur Versöhnung*, Munich, 1989.

——, *Leo Baeck: Teacher of Theresienstadt*, London, 1973.

Fries, H., *Handbuch theologischer Grundbegriffe*, Vol. 2, Munich, 1970.

Geiger, Abraham, *Das Judenthum und seine Geschichte*, Breslau, 1865 (2nd Edition).

Der Gottesdienst des Herzens- Israelitisches Gebetbuch, Nuremberg, 1968.

Graetz, Heinrich, *Volkstümliche Geschichte der Juden*, 3 Vols., Leipzig, 1914.

Graupe, Heinz M., *Die Entstehung des modernen Judentums: Geistesgeschichte der deutschen Juden 1650—1942*, Hamburger Beiträge zur Geschichte der Juden 1, Hamburg, 1969.

Gross, Heinrich, *Die Idee des ewigen und allgemeinen Weltfriedens im Alten Orient und im Alten Testament*, Trier, 1956.

Grunwald, Max, *Monistische Märchen*, Berlin/Vienna, 1921.

Gutbrod, Karl, et al., *Calwer-Bibellexikon*, n.c., 1967.

Heidenheim, W. (trans.), *Die Pessach-Haggada — Erzählung von dem Auszuge Israels aus Ägypten an den beiden ersten Pessach-Abenden*, Basel, n.d.

Herlitz, Georg, et al., *Jüdisches Lexikon*, 5 Vols., Berlin, 1927—1930.

Hertz, J.H., *Pentateuch and Haftorath* (Hebr./Germ./Erl.), Berlin, 1927—1930.

——, *Pentateuch and Haftorahs* (Hebr./Engl./Erl.), London, 1981 (2nd Edition).

Heschel, Abraham J., *The Prophets*, Philadelphia, 1982.

Hirsch, Richard G., *Thy Most Precious Gift — Peace in Jewish Tradition*, New York, 1974.

Hirsch, Samson Raphael, *Israels Gebete*, Frankfurt am Main, 1921 (3rd Edition).

——, *Der Pentateuch* (trans./Erl.), Frankfurt/Main, 1920 (6th Edition).

——, *Die Psalmen*, 2 Parts (trans./Erl.), Frankfurt/Main, 1924.

Homolka, Walter K., "Die frühen Haskala-Bestrebungen in Polen," *Neue Jüdische Nachrichten*, Vol. 5, No. 27, Munich, 1981.

—, "Continuity and Change. Liberal Jewish Theology in a Christian Society," in Walter Homolka and Otto Ziegelmeier (eds.), *Von Wittenberg nach Memphis*, Göttingen, 1989.

—, *From Essence to Existence. Leo Baeck and Religious Identity" Continuity and Change in Liberal and Protestant Theology*, University of London Ph.D. Thesis 1992; Ann Arbor, Michigan, 1993a.

—, "Jewish Religious Identity as a Process of Continuity and Change," in Eckart Bruchner and Geert Vermeire (eds.), *Culturen, Religies en Beeld*, Wielsbeke, 1993b.

—, *Jüdische Identität in der modernen Welt — Leo Baeck und der deutsche Protestantismus*, Gütersloh, 1994.

Husik, Isaac, *A History of Medieval Jewish Philosophy*, New York, 1976.

Isaak, Bernhard, *Der Religionsliberalismus im deutschen Judentum*, unpublished doctoral dissertation, University of Leipzig, 1933.

Jacobs, Louis, *Was Does Judaism Say About . . . ?*, Jerusalem, 1973.

Jerusalem, Wilhelm, *Zu den Menschen eben redet die Geschichte — Preisarbeit No. II der Moritz-Mannheimer-Stiftung der Großloge für Deutschland aus dem Compendium "Friedenspflichten des Einzelnen,"* Gotha, 1917.

The Jewish Encyclopedia, Vol. 9, pp. 565—66, New York/London, 1903.

JONAH (Jews Organized for a Nuclear Arms Halt), *Judaism, Peace and Disarmament — Some Collected Views*, Leeds, 1982.

Jonas, Hans, *Gnosis und spätantiker Geist*, Part 2.1: Gotteserkenntnis, Schau und Vollendung bei Philo von Alexandrien, Göttingen, 1966.

Joseph, Morris, *Judaism as a Creed of Life*, London, 1903.

Kampe, Norbert, "Akademisierung der Juden und Beginn eines studentischen Antisemitismus," in Wolfgang Dreßen (ed.), *Jüdisches Leben*, Berliner Topografien 4, Museumspädagogischer Dienst Berlin — Ästhetik und Kommunikation, Berlin, 1985.

Kaplan, Mordecai M., *Judaism as a Civilization — Toward a Reconstruction of American-Jewish Life*, Philadelphia, 1981.

Karpeles, Gustav (ed.), *Allgemeine Zeitung des Judentums: Ein unparteiisches Organ für alles jüdische Interesse*, No. 63, Berlin, 1899.

Katz, Jacob, *Zur Assimilation und Emanzipation der Juden*, Darmstadt, 1982.

Kautzsch, Emil, et al., *Die Apokryphen und Pseudepigraphen des Alten Testaments*, 2 Vols., Darmstadt, 1975 (4th Edition).

Keeping Posted, *Reconstructionism*, Vol. 27, No. 3, New York, 1982.

—, *Choose Life*, Vol. 28, No. 1, New York, 1982.

Keller, Werner, *Und wurden zerstreut unter alle Völker — Die nach-biblische Geschichte des jüdischen Volkes*, Munich/Zurich, 1966.

Kohler, Kaufmann, *Der Segen Jacobs mit besonderer Berücksichti-gung der alten Versionen und des Midrasch*, Berlin, 1867.

Konkordanz zum Hebräischen Alten Testament, pp. 1436—38, Stuttgart, 1958.

Weltkonkordanz: Praktisches Bibelhandbuch, Katholisches Bibelwerk, Stuttgart, 1968.

Kornfeld, Joseph S., *Judaism and International Peace — Popular Studies in Judaism*, Cincinnati, Ohio, n.d.

Lazarus, Moritz, *Die Ethik des Judenthums*, 2 Vols., Frankfurt/Main, 1904/1911.

Die Lehren des Judentums nach den Quellen, 5 Parts, Verband der deutschen Juden, Leipzig, 1923—1928.

Levi, Guiseppe, *Das Buch der jüdischen Weisheit*, Dreieich, 1980 (3rd Edition).

Levinson, Nathan Peter, "Friede, Friede, aber da ist kein Friede," *Allgemeine Jüdische Wochenzeitung*, Vol. 37, No. 18, Düsseldorf, 1982, p. 3.

Liebeschütz, Hans, *Das Judentum im deutschen Geschichtsbild von Hegel bis Max Weber*, Schriftenreihe wissenschaftlicher Abhandlungen des Leo Baeck Instituts 17, Tübingen, 1967.

Lindeskog, Gösta, *Die Jesusfrage im neuzeitlichen Judentum. Ein Beitrag zur Geschichte der Leben-Jesu-Forschung*, Darmstadt, 1973 (reprint of Uppsala, 1938).

Marx, Gustav, *Die Tötung Ungläubiger nach talmudisch-rabbinis-chem Recht*, Leipzig, 1885.

Mai, G., "Sozialgeschichtliche Bedingungen von Judentum und Antisemitismus im Kaiserreich," in T. Klein, V. Losemann, G. Mai (eds.), *Judentum und Antisemitismus von der Antike bis zur Gegenwart*, Düsseldorf, 1984.

Meecham, Henry G., *The Oldest Version of the Bible: Aristeas on Its Traditional Origin. A Study in Early Apologetic with Translation and Appendices*, London, 1932.

Mekilta de-Rabbi Ishmail, Jacob Z. Lauterbach (ed.), 3 Vols., Philadelphia, 1976.

Melamed, Samual Max, *Theorie, Ursprung und Geschichte der Friedensidee*, Stuttgart, 1909.

Mischnajot: Die sechs Ordnungen der Mischna (Hebr./Germ./Erl.), Basel, 1968 (3rd Edition).

Mommsen, Theodor, *Auch ein Wort über unsere Juden*, Berlin, 1880.

Nestle, Wilhelm, *Der Friedensgedanke in der antiken Welt*, Leipzig, 1938.

Newman, Louis J., *The Talmudic Anthology — Tales and Teachings of the Rabbis*, New York, 1978.

Niewöhner, Friedrich W., "Judentum. Wesen des Judentums," in J. Ritter and K. Gründer (eds.), *Historisches Wörterbuch der Philosophie*, Vol. 4, Darmstadt, 1976.

Nipperday, P. and Rürup, R., "Antisemitismus," in Otto Brunner, Werner Conze, Reinhart Koselleck (eds.), *Geschichtliche Grundbegriffe: Historisches Lexikon zur politisch-sozialen Sprache*, Vol. 1, Stuttgart, 1972.

Paucker, Arnold, "Zur Problematik einer jüdischen Abwehrstrategie in der deutschen Gesellschaft," in Werner E. Mosse (ed.), *Juden im Wilhelminischen Deutschland*, Schriftenreihe wisseschaftlicher Abhandlungen des Leo-Baeck-Instituts 33, Tübingen, 1976.

PHILO-Lexikon — Handbuch des jüdischen Wissens, Berlin, 1935.

Phillipson, M., "Jahresüberblicke," in *Jahrbuch für jüdische Geschichte und Literatur*, Verband der Vereine für jüdische Geschichte und Literatur in Deutschland (ed.), Berlin, 1889ff.

Plaut, Gunther W., *The Rise of Reform Judaism*, New York, 1963/1966.

Prijs, Leo, *Hauptwerke der hebräischen Literatur*, Munich, 1978.

Radday, Yehuda T., *The Unity of Isaiah in the Light of Statistical Linguistics*, Hildesheim, 1973.

Rayner, John D., et al., *Judaism for Today*, London, 1978.

Reinharz, Jehuda, *Fatherland or Promised Land: The Dilemma of the German Jew 1893—1914*, Ann Arbor, MI, 1975.

Richarz, Monika (ed.), *Jüdisches Leben in Deutschland*, 3 vols., Stuttgart, 1976/78/82.

Roche, Peter, Johannes Hoffmann and Walter Homolka (eds.), *Ethische Geldanlagen. Kapital auf neuen Wegen*, Frankfurt am Main, 1992.

Rosenthal, Gilbert S., *Maimonides — His Wisdom for Our Time*, New York, 1969.

—, *The Many Faces of Judaism*, New York, 1978.

Rost, Leonhard, *Einleitung in die alttestamentlichen Apokryphen und Pseudepigraphen einschließlich der großen Qumranhandschriften*, Heidelberg, 1971.

Rürup, Reinhard, "Die 'Judenfrage' der bürgerlichen Gesellschaft und die Entstehung des modernen Antisemitismus," in Reinhard Rürup, *Emanzipation und Antisemitismus: Studien zur 'Judenfrage' der bürgerlichen Gesellschaft*, Kritische Studien zur Geschichtswissenschaft 15, Göttingen, 1975.

Rürup, Reinhard, "Emanzipation und Krise: Zur Geschichte der 'Judenfrage' in Deutschland vor 1890," in Werner E. Mosse and Arnold Paucker (ed.), *Juden im Wilhelminischen Deutschland 1890 — 1914: Ein Sammelband*, Schriftenreihe wissenschaftlicher Abhandlungen des Leo Baeck Instituts 33, Tübingen, 1976.

Scherman, Nossom (trans.), *The Complete ArtScroll Siddur: Weekday, Sabbath, Festival; Nusach Ashkenaz*, New York, 1987 (2nd Edition).

Schmid, Hans Heinrich, *Frieden ohne Illusionen*, Zurich, 1971.

—, *Salôm, "Frieden" im Alten Orient und im Alten Testament*, Stuttgart, 1971.

Schwager, Raymund, *Brauchen wir einen Sündenbock? Gewalt und Erlösung in den biblischen Schriften*, n.c., 1978.

Schwartzman, Sylvan D., *Reform Judaism Then and Now*, New York, 1971.

Seligmann, Caesar, *Geschichte der jüdischen Reformbewegung von Mendelssohn bis zur Gegenwart*, Frankfurt am Main, 1922.

Simon, Ernst Akiva, "Das Zeugnis des Judentums," in *Der Monat, Die großen Kontroversen II*, 1986.

Steck, Odil Hannes, *Friedensvorstellungen im alten Jerusalem*, Zurich, 1972.

Stemberger, Günter, *Geschichte der jüdischen Literatur — Eine Einführung*, Munich, 1977.

Susman, Margarete, *Deutung biblischer Gestalten*, Stuttgart 1955.

Tal, Uriel, *Christians and Jews in Germany: Religion, Politics and Ideology in the Second Reich, 1870—1914*, Ithaca, N.Y./London, 1975.

Toury, Jacob, *Die politischen Orientierungen der Juden in Deutschland: von Jena bis Weimar*, Tübingen, 1966.

Twersky, Isadore (Ed.), *A Maimonides Reader*, New York, 1972.

Union of Liberal and Progressive Synagogues, *Service of the Heart*, London, 1967.

The Universal Jewish Encyclopedia, Vol. 8, pp. 418—421, New York, 1948.

Vogel, Rolf, *Ein Stück von uns — Deutsche Juden in deutschen Armeen 1813—1976,* Mainz, 1977.

Wehler, Hans-Ulrich, *Das Deutsche Kaiserreich 1871—1918,* Deutsche Geschichte 9, Göttingen, 1980 (4th Edition).

Wiener, Max, *Die Anschauungen der Propheten von der Sittlichkeit,* Berlin, 1909.

Wiesel, Elie, *Chassidische Feier,* Vienna, 1974.

—, *Adam oder das Geheimnis des Anfangs,* Freiburg, 1986.

—, *Den Frieden feiern,* Freiburg 1991.

—, "Gleichgültigkeit führt zu Schuld," in *Die Welt,* 27. October 1992.

Wilhelm, Kurt, *Wissenschaft des Judentums im deutschen Sprachbereich: Ein Querschnitt,* Schriftenreihe wissenschaftlicher Abhandlungen des Leo Baeck Instituts 16, 2 Vols., Tübingen, 1967.

Wünsche, August, *Der Jerusalemische Talmud in seinen haggadischen Bestandteilen,* Hildesheim, 1967.

Zunz, Leopold, *Die vierundzwanzig Bücher der Heiligen Schrift,* Basel, 1980.